JAMES HARRINGTON'S REPUBLIC

W. Calvin Dickinson

UNIVERSITY
PRESS OF
AMERICA

Copyright © 1983 by
University Press of America,™ Inc.
P.O. Box 19101, Washington, DC 20036

All rights reserved
Printed in the United States of America

ISBN (Perfect): 0-8191-3020-6
ISBN (Cloth): 0-8191-3019-2

THE POLITICAL PHILOSOPHY OF JAMES HARRINGTON

I. James Harrington

    A. Biography
    B. Influence
    C. Bibliography

II. Modern Prudence: Harrington's Analysis of England's History

    A. Medieval England, 37 a.d. - 1485
    B. Tudor England, 1485 - 1603
    C. Seventeenth Century England

III. Commonwealth of Oceana: Harrington's Constitution for England

    A. Basic Principles
        1. Commonwealth
        2. Agrarian Law
        3. Rotation
    B. Civil Government
        1. Local Administration
        2. Senate and Magistrates
        3. Councils and Dictator
        4. Prerogative Assembly
    C. Religion and Church
    D. Military Establishment
    E. Education System
    F. Summary: The Rota

IV. Appendix

    Government of Oceana Diagram

CHAPTER I

JAMES HARRINGTON (1611-1677)

"No man can be a politician, except he be first an historian or a traveller; for except he can see what must be, or what may be, he is no politician. Now, if he have no knowledge in story, he cannot tell what hath been; and if he hath not been a traveller, he cannot tell what is; but he that neither knoweth what hath been, nor what is, can never tell what must be or what may be."

The Commonwealth of Oceana

BIOGRAPHY

In the century before James Harrington's birth in 1611 momentous changes occurred in English economy and society, and Harrington's family in the sixteenth century was a microcosmic study of those alterations in the larger society of which it was a part. The tumultuous results of the changes occurred during James Harrington's lifetime - in civil war between the classes - and Harrington penned his great work Oceana trying to explain the results to himself and his society. He suggested in his work the solution - or the beneficial result - of the changes which had taken place over a century and a half before 1650.

The economic and social modifications in Tudor England in the sixteenth century involved what Harrington called in Oceana a change in the "balance of property." The first Tudor monarch, Henry VII, broke up some noble estates with the statutes of population, retainers, and alienation. The middle class became more prosperous through their own endeavors and through the sponsorship of the king. With their newly acquired wealth they could take advantage of the new land market. Land was now seen as a marketable item rather than as merely a seat of power and prestige, as it had been viewed in the Middle Ages. The capitalists in the middle class began to use money acquired through trade or profession to purchase property as an investment as well as a mark of social prestige. Henry VIII provided more land for purchase by the middle class when he confiscated church properties in England during the religious reformation of the 1530's. Henry kept some of the church lands for himself, but most of it was granted or sold. Peers received relatively little of the property; the great bulk of it went to commoners - courtiers, military officers, knights, esquires, gentlemen, lawyers, physicians, merchants.[1] This clever move on the part of the king bound these English citizens to support him against the resurgence of the Catholic Church, but, according to Harrington's later interpretation of history, it also contributed to the change in balance of property which would destroy Charles I in the 1640's.

Harrington's family was involved in this change in the balance of property; the Harrington family was one of those which gained property, prestige, and privilege in the exchange. Robert Harrington became the first of his immediate family to hold the office of High Sheriff of Rutlandshire in 1492; five other Harringtons held the title by the seventeenth century. During this time the family, by a successful series of land purchases and marriage settlements, acquired "one of the largest landed fortunes in England."[2] James Harrington's ancestor, Sir James of Exton (1511-1592), added five large manors to the family estates during his lifetime. Sir James's eleven children married well, and his descendents included eight dukes, three marquises, several earls, nine counts, twenty-seven viscounts, and thirty-six barons.[3] Another relative of our James Harrington, Sir John of Kelston (1561-1612), was "the most famous of the Harringtons;"[4] he invented the water closet (commode), and his name presumably gave that appliance its cherished nickname, "john." This John was a godson to Queen Elizabeth. Thus the rise of the Harrington family illustrated the change in balance of property that James Harrington later described.

James Harrington was born to Sir Sapcote Harrington and his wife in 1611. Sir Sapcote was a grandson of Sir James of Exton. He must have been comfortably wealthy, for he died in 1630 and left his entire fortune to his eldest son, James, who was able to live well for the remainder of his life without working. He was also able to support partially three brothers and four sisters.

James's formal education was brief, consisting of only two or three years in Trinity College, Oxford. He enrolled in 1629, but left without taking a degree. In 1631 he enrolled in Middle Temple, a law school, but abandoned this after only a few weeks. Despite his apparent disdain for formal education, he saw its importance in the life of a state, for his suggested school system occupied considerable space in Oceana. In spite of his abandoning formal education, learning was evidently the most important guide in Harrington's life and thought. The philosophy and ideas in Oceana flowed directly out of his life-long learning experience. His writings displayed a huge store of knowledge in Harrington's mind, and the ways he used this storehouse showed that he considered knowledge, particularly history, the most important consideration in decisions about the affairs of present time.

Harrington's command of knowledge is impressive even in the twentieth century. He mastered several languages, ancient as well as modern. His command of literature, and especially of the Bible, was extensive. But it was his knowledge of ancient and modern history that is most impressive. Harrington used history as the building material for his political philosophy. He dipped back into recent as well as ancient history to find examples which would instruct him as to the most efficient elements of government for man. He did not, as Thomas Hobbes did a few years before him, and John Locke did a few years after him, construct his political philosophy completely out of his mind in the deductive method. He used inductive reasoning, as modern scientists do, in citing historical experiments to construct most of his government. In his emphasis on history Harrington followed the Italian Machiavelli, "whose books are neglected."[5]

One of the most amazing aspects of Harrington's interpretation of history was his detachment from the times in which he lived, so that he was able to look at the civil wars of the 1640's with a cool, analytical, and unemotional eye. Even more amazing, he was able to interpret the causes of the civil wars in the same way that some historians have in the twentieth century. He did not see them as struggles between patriots and brigands; nor did he see them as conflicts between the "right" church and the "wrong" religious group. In a sophisticated manner Harrington saw the civil wars as part of a long-time development in England in which changes were taking place in the economic and social relationships of the population. He traced the development back to the reign of Henry VII and the property changes that began to take place at that time. Property began to move out of the hands of the nobility and into the possession of the middle class. The movement continued, and by the middle of the seventeenth century the new property-owning middle class demanded its proper social and constitutional positions because of its economic position.

In making economics the determining factor in the development of history and in showing that history was moving toward a goal, which was the development of a utopia that would stop the flow of history, Harrington was anticipating the nineteenth century philosophy of history that Karl Marx constructed. With his statement "such as is the proportion or balance of dominion or property in land, such is the nature of the empire,"[6] Harrington preceded Marx by two hundred years in declaring that the distribution of wealth determines the type of government - monarchy, aristocracy, democracy - that develops. A major difference between Harrington and Marx was that Harrington lived in an agricultural economy in England and Marx lived in an industrial economy in Germany and England. Therefore Harrington saw the importance only of wealth in land and Marx saw only the importance of industrial wealth. Another major philosophical difference in the two men was the conception of class struggle. Marx saw this antagonism as "the motive force in history;" Harrington placed very little emphasis on class antagonism.[7] Both of them, however, saw the control of the state by those who controlled the wealth, and both saw the structure of the state changing through history as the control of wealth changed. Both also saw the development of history ending or culminating in the establishment of the ideal state - a republic for Harrington and a communist society for Marx.

In addition to his extensive knowledge acquired from books, Harrington's education was extended by his travels in Europe. The Grand Tour of Europe was a customary practice for young men of the upper class at this time and was intended to introduce them to the sophisticated adult world of the Continent. It did provide excellent opportunities for opening his mind and broadening his perspective, but probably few received as much education from the experience as did Harrington. That he realized the significance of travel in his own education, and that he highly recommended it for others' education is obvious in this quotation from Oceana:

> No man can be a politician except he be first

an Historian or a traveller; for except he can
see what Must be, or May be, he is no politician;
Now if he have no knowledge in story, he cannot
tell what hath been; and if he hath not been a
traveller, he cannot tell what is; but he that
neither knoweth what hath been, nor what is; can
never tell what must be, or what may be.[8]

Harrington's grand tour, beginning in 1632, took
him to the Netherlands, to Denmark, to France, to Italy.
He may have served with an English military regiment in
the Netherlands; he observed the shaping of absolute
monarchy by Louis XIII and Richelieu in France; and he
admired the process of balloting in Venice, Italy.
There is no question that the government of Venice impressed him more than any of the others, for it was the
practices of this government that he copied to some extent for England in his <u>Oceana</u>. His biographer William
Toland said that "he prefer's Venice to all other places
in Italy, as he did its Government to all those of the
whole World."[9] With an imperfect knowledge of the
Venetian government, Harrington mistakenly thought that
it was both democratic and stable. Desiring these
characteristics for English government, he copied
Venetian institutions in his <u>Oceana</u>.

Having learned in his travels about types of
governments ranging from absolute monarchy in France to
republican in Venice, Harrington returned to England in
the 1630's to find its government being destroyed by
conflict. As the perpetual student, Harrington began
to view this conflict from the outside, taking almost
no part in it, but acting as an objective observer
trying to understand its causes. To his observations
he added the extensive knowledge that he had acquired
from books and from his travels. From these sources
he produced both the explanation for the conflict and
civil wars as well as the solution in the form of perfect government. His explanation of the causes and
his solution to the problems were published in 1656 in
<u>Oceana</u>.

When the problems between King Charles I and his
country exploded in civil war in the 1640's, Harrington
was a close observer. Although he assumed no military
role during the wars, he did lend the government money
in 1641 and 1642, and in 1645 he raised money for the
Parliament. Harrington supported, in these ways, the
rebels or roundheads during the wars. During the king's

captivity by the Parliament in 1647, Harrington was chosen Groom of the Bedchamber, a position which made him a frequent companion of the captive king. Harrington was by this time convinced that England must establish a republican form of government, and according to his biographer John Aubrey, Harrington repeatedly attempted to convert the king to his point of view. Aubrey said that "the king loved his company; only he would not endure to heare of a Commonwealth /republic/; and Mr. Harrington passionately loved his Majestie."[10]

There is some controversy among historians as to whether Harrington witnessed Charles' execution in 1649. One of Harrington's relatives said, "Youself was caressed by the blessed martyr Charles, and honoured with his words, and even his princely favours from his own hands on the scaffold;"[11] but J.G.A. Pocock[12] cast doubt on Harrington's presence at the decapitation. Nevertheless, Charles's death "gave him so great a griefe"[13] that Harrington withdrew from society for some time and started composing Oceana in 1654.

Harrington's reasons for writing Oceana can only be supposed. He did dedicate the book to Oliver Cromwell, ruler of England in 1656, the year that Oceana was published. It might be supposed from this dedication that Harrington hoped Cromwell would adopt Oceana and would actually create the government that Harrington outlined in the book; but this was not to be. Cromwell's secret service actually seized Oceana as it was being printed, and it took a personal appeal by Harrington to Cromwell's daughter to have the book released for publication and sale. So Cromwell was suspicious of, rather than accepting of, the book. Later, Harrington made an attempt to persuade the government to accept his ideas after Cromwell's death.

In 1659, a year after Cromwell's death, Harrington launched a full-scale campaign to make his ideas popular and to have them accepted. He wrote a number of publications explaining Oceana, including Aphorisms Political, The Art of Lawgiving and Brief Directions. In July a document called "Humble Petititon of Divers Well-Affected Persons," which contained Harrington's ideas, was presented to Parliament by Harrington's friend Henry Nevill. The petition may have been written by Harrington, for it outlined six steps by which England could establish the government that Harrington prescribed. Parliament expressed thanks for the document and apparently never considered it again.

Harrington's most successful effort to popularize his ideas in 1659 involved the establishment of the Rota Club. This debate club met at various coffeehouses, popular gathering places where persons met to sip the new drink introduced into Europe in the seventeenth century. The Turke's Head was a meeting place for the Rota Club; it installed "A large ovall-table, with a passage in the middle for Miles to deliver his Coffee."[14] Harrington and his disciples sat around this table to discuss his ideas and drink coffee. There was no closed membership in the Rota; all were invited to participate, and many did. One of the major points of interest in the Rota was the ballot box, used to decide the winner in each night's debate. This gimmick grew large crowds for the debate contests and created interest in Harrington's ideas, for the ballot box was an important part of Harrington's government.

The year 1660 brought an abrupt change in Harrington's popularity, life, and fortune. General Monk returned from Scotland at the head of his army to dissolve the Parliament and invite Charles II to return to England as king. The Rota Club disappeared. Harrington was committed to the Tower of London as a prisoner of Charles II in 1661 because of his republican activities. After months in confinement Harrington was released as a result of efforts by his family and because of his seriously deteriorating health.

In retirement in London, with broken health and disturbed mind, Harrington married his former sweetheart, "a comely and discreete ladie." Harrington was sixty-four at the time of his marriage and in poor health, so "he would never lye with her, but loved and admired her dearly."[15]

In 1677 Harrington died, having lost his "memorie and discourse" about a year before his death.[16]

INFLUENCE

Despite the vigorous efforts of Harrington on behalf of his philosophy of government, despite the spirit of experimentation which was in the air in the 1650's, and despite the intense popularity of Harrington's Rota Club in 1659, the philosophy of <u>Oceana</u> was not adopted by England in the seventeenth century. Charles II returned to rule a different England than Harrington proposed. Nevertheless, Harrington prevailed in the long run. England adopted many of his individual ideas in succeeding centuries, and the United States adopted them in a more comprehensive way. Had Harrington lived to see the individual states created, and then the United States formed, he would have been especially pleased with the developments. Harrington, though he is less studied in American schools than Locke, Montesquieu, and Rousseau, stands at least as tall as these other European philosophers in the influence that he has exerted on the political development of America.

It is not surprising that Harrington failed to convince the English ruling class to adopt his republican government. England had been ruled by kings since the Anglo-Saxon period, and any type non-monarchical government would have been alien to the history of the country. On the other hand, the experiment with non-monarchical government in the 1650's had been very unsatisfactory to the English ruling class, and by 1659 they were ready to return to monarchy, a form of government familiar to them. It is not surprising that they rejected Harrington's republic, along with its written constitution, its balance of property concept, and its office rotation system; it is not surprising that they invited Charles II in 1660 to return to England and reestablish the monarchy.

Charles II did not, however return to the England of old. The civil wars of the 1640's and the republican experiments of the 1650's had changed the country so greatly that it would never return to its former style of monarchy. Charles would rule with more limited authority than did his predecessors, and in time the government would be even more liberalized. Some of Harrington's ideas would be adopted individually, but not as a system. This subsequent history has shown that Harrington was wrong in thinking that the economic situation in England would no longer tolerate monarchy but he was correct in his basic assumption that any form of government must eventually accommodate itself to the economic power of the population.

Chronologically, the first idea of Harrington that England adopted was religious toleration. It existed in England at the same time Harrington prescribed it in Oceana. The Instrument of Government (1653) and the Humble Petition and Advice (1657) contained provisions for limited toleration. In 1689 the Toleration Act passed both houses of Parliament rather easily and was readily signed by William III. It allowed religious worship for non-conformists, but barred them from government offices. Harrington would not have approved that restriction: "Men who have the means to assert liberty of conscience have the means to assert civil liberty; and will do it if they are oppressed in their consciences."[17] Harrington did exclude Jews and Roman Catholics from freedom of worship, as did the Toleration Act of 1689.

Extension of the franchise, which Harrington gave to all men in the commonwealth who were not servants, came to England in the nineteenth century. The Reform Act of 1832 extended the franchise for the first time since 1430 in the counties, and additional acts in 1867, 1884, 1918, 1928, and 1970 completed the move toward political democracy. Harrington would have never gone this far, but he was ahead of his time in 1656.

State-financed education was an idea of Harrington's which England adopted in isolated instances in the 1650's. In 1833, with a government grant of £20,000 a year for the support of elementary education, the English government began its permanent financing of education. Harrington outlined a system of free schools and compulsory education in Oceana for males only. Like most persons of any time, Harrington was a product of his own time, and female education and suffrage were not contemporary ideas.

The secret vote, or Australian ballot, was another part of Harrington's Oceana that England adopted, this one in 1872 through the Ballot Act. Harrington used the voting process of the city of Venice as a model for his system, which he laid out in a long treatise called "The Manner and Use of the Ballot." His purpose for the secret ballot in Oceana was the same as that of the Ballot Act of 1872 - to control corruption, bribery, and coercion. There was an obvious interest in this mechanism in seventeenth century England, as exhibited in the crowds that gathered daily to watch the working of the "balloting box" at the Rota Club meetings.

England, with its long history of monarchical government and its unsatisfactory seventeenth century experiments with republicanism, did not adopt wholesale the Oceana of James Harrington, but, as outlined above, it did adopt some of the individual ideas of Harrington, whether the practice sprang immediately from Harrington's influence or not. North America, however, in seeking to break with England was fertile ground for Harrington's philosophy. As H. F. Russell-Smith so poetically put it in his book on Harrington: "To receive embodiment in practice the theories of the Commonwealth had to be conveyed to infant states across the Atlantic."[18] North American political ground was plowed in the seventeenth century, when Harrington was preparing his seeds, and North America was ready to be planted with his ideas. We should remember that many of the people who settled North America were dissatisfied with the British system of government and were searching for new ideas. Harrington's ideas were among those accepted more completely in North America than in England.

Many Americans in the seventeenth century had shared common experiences with James Harrington. Before they had come to the American colonies, many had lived in England at the same time as had Harrington, and many had experienced the civil wars that had been so influential with Harrington. They may have read the same books and traveled in Europe as did Harrington. Therefore, many Americans' minds were formed by the same influences that determined Harrington's ideas. Many Americans obviously read Harrington's Oceana after it was published in 1656, and many Americans obviously agreed with the ideas in the book because their backgrounds and experiences had been similar to Harrington's.

A number of copies of Oceana dating from colonial times still exist in libraries in the United States, so the number existant during colonial times must have been substantially greater. William Penn's secretary of state had a copy of Oceana, and Penn might well have had one also, but his library has been lost. The Library Company of Philadelphia had three copies of Oceana. Harvard College possessed a copy after 1722. Robert Hunter, governor of New York colony, had a copy, and James Otis, colonial lawyer, indicated that he had read Harrington. Finally, at least two of the most important fathers of our country owned copies of Oceana. John Adams, delegate to the Continental Congresses and second President of the United States, owned two copies. As the principal author of the Massachusetts Constitution of 1780, Adams used Harrington's ideas in the document. Thomas Jefferson, third President of the United States, may have used Locke's ideas in his Declaration of Independence, but he also owned a copy of Harrington's <u>Oceana</u>, which can still be seen in the Library of Congress. Similarities between Jefferson's and Harrington's ideas will be noted later.

Harrington's ideas were influential in at least four constitutions of American colonies. The Fundamental Constitutions of Carolina, in effect after 1669, may have been written by John Locke; but if Locke did compose the document, he was using some of the ideas of Harrington. William Penn's colonies, New Jersey and Pennsylvania, both used <u>Oceana</u> in forming their constitutions, and Massachusetts's constitution of 1780 was an example of Harrington's influence, as mentioned above.[20]

Harrington foresaw the American Revolution by applying the principles of his philosophy to the development of empires. He viewed the colonies that England possessed during his lifetime, and he applied his philosophy of economics determining history to them, predicting revolt. "The colonys in the Indies, they are yet babes that cannot live without sucking the breasts of their mother-citys, but such as I mistake, if when they come of age they do not wean themselves."[21] He predicted that if the mother country gave the colonial landowners control over their own affairs, "that would bring the government from provincial and dependent to national and independent."[22] So he was correctly prophesying from his knowledge of history the development of the American Revolution a hundred years later.

Harrington's ideas which were adopted by the United States number at least thirteen. Important principles in Harrington's scheme which did not become a part of this country's government were his agrarian law, his separation of debate and vote between the houses of the legislature, his state church, and his dictator provision. Most of the other ideas of Harrington will be very familiar to an American, even though they were stated in his stilted, dull, and repetitous writing style.

Harrington's state was to be governed by a <u>written</u> constitution, an idea alien to English history. Never had England been governed by one document until Harrington's own time, when the Instrument of Government acted as a constitution in the 1650's. This document was discarded before the end of the decade, and never

11

again has England lived under a written constitution. The United States, on the other hand, embraced the idea of a written constitution one hundred years later, adopting the Articles of Confederation as its first constitution in 1781 and adopting the present Constitution in 1789. Harrington's constitution was written in <u>The Model of the Commonwealth of Oceana</u>, composed in thirty "orders." All other of Harrington's writings were explanation, elaboration, and defense of <u>The Model</u>.

Another Harrington idea alien to English history that the Americans saw wisdom in was separation of powers. English government operated under the idea of unified power - the "king's government." This developed from the ancient custom of the king's household acting as the government. The servants in the household were the king's servants, and the decision-making power in the household was the king's. As the English government grew beyond the household it was still the king's government, paid for and dominated by the king. As a result of American problems with the English government in the eighteenth century, Americans reacted against the idea of lodging all power within one person or one part of the government. So Americans separated power in the Constitution of 1787 into three branches of government. Harrington separated the powers of government into two branches, legislative and judicial; but he did not absolutely separate legislative and judicial functions, as Montesquieu did in <u>The Spirit of Laws</u>, and as Americans did in the <u>Constitution of 1787</u>. Harrington allowed the legislature to exercise some judicial power, as was customary in English history.[23]

The bicameral legislative branch was a tradition in England, at least since the fourteenth century. Harrington continued the tradition with this reasoning: "A popular assembly without a senate cannot be wise. A senate without a popular assembly will not be honest."[24] Harrington's bicameral Parliament was different from the traditional English institution in that he abolished the peerage, and therefore the House of Lords, substituting instead the Senate. England had abolished her House of Lords in 1649, and had substituted a second house without nobles in 1657, so Harrington was reflecting contemporary trends in England when he continued the bicameral legislature without a house of peers. His rationale with the two-house legislature was not, however, merely to reflect current events, but to provide an honest, effective, and popular legislature. John Adams, a student of Harrington, has been given credit for the predominance of the bicameral legislature in the United States.[25] The particular form that it took came as a result of the Connecticut Compromise in the Constitutional Convention of 1787.

Harrington employed the check and balance system so familiar to all Americans in his separation of powers and in his arrangement of the bicameral Parliament. "The right of debate . . . be wholly and only in the senate, without any power at all of result /vote/." . . . the power of result /vote/ be wholly and only in the people /assembly/, without any right at all of debate."[26] He thought that "a popular assembly, . . . is not capable of any prudent debate," and "a senate, rightly constituted for debate, must consist of so few and eminent persons that, if they have the result /vote/ too, they will not resolve according unto the interest of the people, but according to the interest of themselves."[27] Americans did not employ this particular mechanism of check and balance, and Harrington did not employ as elaborate a system of checks and balances as the Americans wrote into their constitution, but the principle of one part of the government checking the potential weaknesses of another was definitely present in Harrington's Oceana.

Another form of check on the abuse of power that Harrington employed was short tenure for officeholders. Members of the Senate and Assembly were elected for three year terms. In periods of emergency the Council of War could become Dictator, but only for three months. This briefness of terms is emphasized when compared with the lifetime tenure for members of the House of Lords and the indefinite terms for members of the House of Commons, which was the tradition in English history. Harrington obviously feared, as his critic John Milton charged, "that long continuance of power may corrupt sincerest men,"[28] and he hoped that short tenure would diminish such corruption. Harrington was not as severe concerning tenure of office as the English Chartists of the nineteenth century, who demanded that tenure of office for members of Parliament last only one year. The Americans used six years for Senators, two years for Representatives, and four years for Presidents. Some states allowed only one term for governors.

Closely connected with short tenure of office was Harrington's famous idea of rotation in office. One-third of the Legislature of Oceana was to be retired annually, leaving two-thirds to carry on with a new one-third elected each year. Harrington illustrated the value of this arrangement with a metaphor: "An assembly continued by succession or due rotation . . . grows up and is like a man who, though he change his flesh, neither changeth his body nor his soul."[29] John Milton criticized rotation in office, "as having too much affinity with the wheel of fortune."[30] Harrington thought that the element of chance in electing new members was overcome by the danger of "prolongation of magistracy."[31] Harrington wanted the people to literally participate in the government, to "pour themselves in."[32] The constitutional fathers of the United States obviously agreed with Harrington's reasoning, copying him exactly in rotating one-third of the Senate membership every election. President Andrew Jackson practiced the idea of rotation, too, with his infamous "spoils system," rotating personnel in and out of the government bureaucracy in the belief that all citizens could and should serve in the government. Rotation is also practiced by the United States and the various state governments in limiting the terms of Presidents and governors.

In order to keep the law in accordance with the will of the people, Harrington introduced an unusual type of referendum in Oceana. Every piece of proposed legislation had to be "printed and published to the whole nation, six weeks before the time that the representative is to assemble and give the vote of the commonwealth." Then, he said, "This representative is nothing else but an instrument or method, whereby to receive the result of the whole nation."[33] In this way the people had to accept legislation before it was passed, or unpopular legislation did not become law. Although the United States government does not practice the referendum, except in the cases of amendments to the Constitution, several states allow referendums.

Harrington's wide extension of the suffrage was copied in the United States, but at about the same time that England was also extending the vote, as noted above. Voting standards in America were controlled by the states, and most of the states used property requirements in their standards in the eighteenth and early nineteenth centuries. About 1830, as in England, the states liberalized their voting laws.

The United States was afraid of full democracy in the eighteenth century, as was Harrington. The United States, like Harrington, used indirect election to weaken the sovereignty of the people. Harrington used an elaborate system of indirect election for his legislators; the United States Constitution employed indirect election methods for President and for Senators. The Electoral College still exists to prevent the people from voting directly for the President, but the Sixteenth Amendment in 1913 provided for direct election of Senators.

The secret ballot, outlined in Harrington's <u>Oceana</u>, and provided in England in 1872, has become a part of American voting procedure. The value of secret ballot was recognized in all three cases. To use Harrington's words: "If your suffrage be barefaced, I dare say you shall not have one fair /vote/ cast in twenty. But whatever a man's fortune be at the /ballot/ box, he neither knoweth whom to thank nor whom to challenge."[34]

Outside the organization of the government, the United States has followed several ideas that Harrington suggested in <u>Oceana</u>. Religious toleration was one of the most important. Thomas Jefferson, who is known to have studied Harrington's ideas, was so proud of helping make religious toleration a part of our society that he had this achievement carved on his tombstone. The United States did differ from England, and from Harrington's <u>Oceana</u>, in not supporting a state church. As a matter of fact, the First Amendment forbade any connection between church and state. The United States went further than Harrington in separating church and state, but the United States did use Harrington's wisdom, and the wisdom of the eighteenth century, in allowing religious differentiation.

Harrington advocated free public education, calling for a free school in each one of the "tribes" of the country. Education was compulsory for children nine through fifteen in families which had more than one child. Tuition was to be paid if the family could afford it; education was free to those who could not. America was experimenting with public education at the same time that Harrington suggested the idea. In 1647 Massachusetts required all towns of fifty families to maintain a teacher, and all towns of one hundred families were required to establish a grammar school. The schools could be either tax-supported or fee-supported.

Other New England colonies passed similar laws. By 1817 Jefferson, an admirer of Harrington, had developed a complete plan for public education in Virginia. He proposed free elementary and high schools throughout the state, but he did not require compulsory attendance. The legislature rejected his plan, but in 1818 it did provide $45,000 for elementary education. In 1834 Pennsylvania passed a Free School Act, and in 1837 Massachusetts created a State Board of Education. Generally public education developed in the South after the Civil War.

Lastly, America inherited Harrington's aversion to the age-honored laws of primogeniture (eldest son inheriting all his father's property). He criticized laws of primogeniture as "a flinty custom."[35] Agreeing with the Diggers' condemnation of these laws, Harrington made equal distribution of property among heirs one of the cornerstones of his philosophy. Indeed, distribution of property somewhat equally among heirs was the heart of Harrington's famous Agrarian Law: Fathers "having more than one son, shall leave his lands either equally divided among them, . . . or so near equally, ... that the greater part or portion of the same remaining unto the eldest exceed not the value of two thousand pounds revenue."[36] Thomas Jefferson despised laws of primogeniture as much as did Harrington. Jefferson called the abolition of primogeniture, which he spearheaded in Virginia, "the best of all Agrarian Laws," and he thought that abolition of primogeniture was one of the four great preservers of liberty and democracy.[37] The American states followed Harrington's and Jefferson's admonitions and abolished primogeniture after the revolution.

The numerous examples cited above are convincing evidence that Harrington's ideas were influential in the eighteenth century and later. The reason that these ideas quickly became important and are still influential today is that we are still in the period of historical development that was being forged in Harrington's time. His importance is that he was able to recognize early the trends that were developing. He could see them in the history of his country; he could see them in the history of his family; and he could see them in the events of his lifetime. He had an extraordinary sense of history, and he was able to use this ability to understand the events of his own time.

Harrington abandoned the appeal to authority of the Scripture, he abandoned the appeal to nature, and he abandoned the appeal to syllogistic logic to find the explanations and the answers to the problems of his time. Other philosophers and political scientists of his time and before were utilizing these approaches. Harrington instead appealed to history for his explanations and his answers. He correctly sought to find in the past the reasons for the problems of the present; and he sought to find in experience of the past the answers to the problems of the present.

Harrington was not the only one to suggest each of these ideas, nor was he the first one to suggest each of them. This acknowledgement indicates that Harrington was a product of the history that he attempted to use. The same historical forces that influenced Harrington had also operated on other peoples' minds so that similar ideas and conclusions developed from similar events and trends in different people's minds.

The fact that Harrington's ideas still influence the western world three hundred years after his death is an indication that we are still in the same historical period and an indication that Harrington correctly read and interpreted the historical principles of this period. Harrington is not important because he was powerful in his own time; he is important because of his influence on times after his own.

FOOTNOTES

[1] John Mackie, The Earlier Tudors (Oxford, Clarendon Press, 1952), pp. 400-401.

[2] Ian Grimble, The Harrington Family (London: Jonathan Cape, 1957), p. 65.

[3] Charles Blitzer, Immortal Commonwealth (New Haven, Archon, 1960), pp. 6-7.

[4] Ibid., p. 8.

[5] James Harrington, The Commonwealth of Oceana, in The Political Works of James Harrington, J.G.A. Pocock (ed.), (Cambridge: University Press, 1977), p. 161. (All subsequent citations of Harrington are taken from this edition.).

[6] Harrington, Oceana, p. 163.

[7] Christopher Hill, Puritanism and Revolution (New York: Schocken, 1964), p. 312.

[8] Harrington, Oceana, p. 310.

[9] John Toland, The Oceana of James Harrington and His Other Works (London: 1747), p. xv.

[10] John Aubrey, Brief Lives, O. L. Dick (ed.), (Ann Arbor, 1957), p. 124.

[11] Grimble, Harington Family, p. 13.

[12] Pocock, Political Works, p. 4.

[13] Aubrey, Brief Lives, p. 124.

[14] Ibid., p. 125.

[15] Ibid., p. 126.

[16] Ibid., p. 127.

[17] Harrington, System of Politics, p. 844.

[18] H. F. Russell Smith, Harrington and His Oceana (New York: Octagon Books, 1971), p. 121.

[19] Ibid., p. 153.

[20] Ibid., Chapter VII.

[21] Harrington, Oceana, pp. 168-169.

[22] Ibid., p. 167.

[23] Ibid., pp. 281-282.

[24] Harrington, Aphorisms Political, pp. 711-772.

[25] Russell Smith, Harrington, p. 199.
[26] Harrington, The Art of Lawgiving, p. 674.
[27] Harrington, Aphorisms Political, p. 771.
[28] John Milton, The Ready and Easy Way to Establish a Free Commonwealth (London, 1660).
[29] Harrington, Prerogative of Popular Government, p. 494
[30] Milton, Ready and Easy Way.
[31] Harrington, Prerogative of Popular Government, p. 473
[32] Harrington, Oceana, p. 245.
[33] Harrington, Valerius and Publicola, pp. 799, 800.
[34] Harrington, Oceana, p. 244.
[35] Ibid., p. 237.
[36] Ibid., p. 231.
[37] Russell Smith, Harrington, p. 200.

BIBLIOGRAPHY

HARRINGTON'S WORKS CITED

The Commonwealth of Oceana, 1656.

The Prerogative of Popular Government, 1658.

Aphorisms Political, 1659.

The Art of Lawgiving, 1659.

Brief Directions, 1659.

Valerius and Publicola, 1659.

The Manner and Use of the Ballot, 1660.

The Rota, 1660.

A System of Politics, c. 1661.

WORKS ABOUT HARRINGTON

Aubrey, John Brief Lives. Ed., O. L. Dick, Ann Arbor, 1957.

Blitzer, Charles. Immortal Commonwealth, New Haven, 1960.

Dow, John G. "The Political Ideal of the English Commonwealth," *English Historical Reivew*, VI (April, 1891), pp. 306-330.

Downs, Michael. *James Harrington*, Boston, 1977.

Dwight, Theodore. "James Harrington and His Influence Upon American Political Institutions and Political Thought," *Political Science Quarterly*, II (1887), pp. 1-45.

Gooch, G. P. *English Democratic Ideas in the Seventeenth Century*, Cambridge, 1954.

Gough, J. W. "Harrington and Contemporary Thought," *Political Science Quarterly*, XLV (1930), pp. 395-404.

Grimble, Ian. *The Harington Family*, London, 1957.

Levett, H. E. "James Harrington," *Social and Political Ideas of the Sixteenth and Seventeenth Centuries*, Ed., F. J. C. Hearnshaw, New York, 1949.

MacPherson, C. G. *The Political Theory of Possessive Individualism: Hobbes to Locke*, Oxford, 1962.

Russell Smith, H. F. *Harrington and His Oceana*, New York, 1971.

Shklar, Judith N. "Ideology Hunting: The Case of James Harrington," *American Political Science Review*, XIII (1959), pp. 662-692.

Tawney, R. H. "Harrington's Interpretation of His Age," *Proceedings of the British Academy*, XXVII (1941), pp. 200-223.

Zagorin, Perez. *Political Thought in the English Revolution*, London, 1954.

CHAPTER II

MODERN PRUDENCE:

HARRINGTON'S ANALYSIS OF ENGLAND'S HISTORY

"The monarchy of England was not a government by arms, but a government by laws, though imperfect or ineffectual laws."

Aphorisms Political

The following selection is taken from Harrington's <u>Commonwealth</u> <u>of</u> <u>Oceana</u>, "The Second Part of the Preliminaries." In the first section of "The Preliminaries" he set out his "principles of government," emphasizing the idea that power in government should be related to control of land. In "The Second Part" he dealt with the history of England, interpreting it as the story of a relationship between land ownership and government stability. He substituted fictitious for proper names in English history, supposedly because of his fear of censorship. The editor will supply the correct names in brackets beside the fictitious ones.

MEDIEVAL ENGLAND

The constitution of the late monarchy of Oceana is to be considered in relation unto the different nations, by whom it hath been successively subdued and governed. The first of these were the Romans, the second the Teutons [Saxons], the third the Scandians [Danes], and the fourth the Neustrians [Normans].

The government of the Romans, who held it as a province, I shall omit because I am to speak of their provincial government in another place; only it is to be remembered in this that if we have given over running up and down naked and with dappled hides, learned to write and read, to be instructed with good arts, for all these we are beholding to the Romans either immediately, or mediately by the Teutons [Saxons]; for that the Teutons had the arts from no other hand is plain enough by their language, which hath yet no word to signify either writing or reading but what is derived from the Latin. Furthermore, by the help of these arts so learned, we have been capable of that religion which we have long since received; wherefore it seemeth unto me that we ought not to detract from the memory of the Romans, by whose means we are as it were of beasts become men, and by whose means we might yet of obscure and ignorant men (if we thought not too well of ourselves) become a wise and a great people.

The Romans having governed Oceana /England/ provincially, the Teutons /Saxons/ were the first that introduced the form of the late monarchy; to these succeeded the Scandians /Danes/, of whom (because their reign was short, as also because they made little alteration in the government as to the form) I shall take no notice. But the Teutons /Saxons/, going to work upon the Gothic balance /Feudalism/, divided the whole nation into three sorts of feuds, that of ealdorman, that of king's thane, and that of middle thane.

When the kingdom was first divided into precincts will be as hard to show as when it began first to be governed; it being impossible that there should be any government without some division. The division that was in use with the Teutons /Saxons/ was by counties, and every county had either its ealdorman, or high reeve. The title of Ealdorman came in time to eorl, or erle, and that of high reeve to high sheriff.

Earl of the shire or county denoted the king's thane, or tenant by grant serjeantry, or knight's service in chief or *in capite*; his possessions were sometimes the whole territory, from whence he had his denomination, that is the whole country, sometimes more than one county and sometimes less, the remaining part being in the crown. He had also sometimes a third, or some other customary part of the profits of certain cities, boroughs or other places within his earldom. For an example of the possessions of earls in ancient times, Ethelred had unto him and his heirs the whole kingdom of Mercia, containing three or four counties; and there were others that had little less.

'King's thane' was also an honorary title, unto which he was qualified that had five hides of land held immediately of the king by service of personal attendance; insomuch that if a churl or country man had thriven unto this proportion, having a church, a kitchen, a bell house (that is a hall with a bell in it to call his family to dinner), a borough gate with a seat (that is a porch) of his own, and any distinct office in the king's court, then was he the king's thane. But the proportion of any hide land, otherwise called <u>caruca</u>, or a ploughland, is difficult to understand, because it was not certain; nevertheless it is generally conceived to be so much as may be managed with one plough, and would yield the maintenance of the same with the appurtenances in all kinds.

The middle thane was feudal, but not honorary; he was also called a vavasor, and his lands a vavasory, which held of some mesne lord, and not immediately of the king.

Possessions and their tenures, being of this nature, show the balance of the Teuton monarchy; wherein the riches of earls were so vast, that to arise from the balance of their dominion unto their power, they were not only called <u>reguli</u> or little kings, but were such indeed, their jurisdiction being of two sorts, either that which was exercised by them in the court of their counties, or in the high court of the kingdom.

In the territory dominating an earl, if it were all his own, the courts held, and the profits of that jurisdiction, were to his own use and benefit. But if he had but some part of his county, this his jurisdiction and courts (saving perhaps in those possessions that were his own) were held by him to the king's use and benefit; that is, he commonly supplied the office with the sheriffs regularly executed in countries that had no earls, and whence they came to be called <u>vicecomites</u>. The court of the county that had an earl was held by the earl and the bishop of the diocese, after the manner of the sheriff's tourns unto this day, by which means both the ecclesiastical and temporal laws were given in charge together unto the country; the causes of vavasors of vavasories appertained to the cognisance of this court, where wills were proved, judgment and execution given, cases criminal and civil determined.

The king's thanes had like jurisdiction in their thane-lands as lords in their manors, where they also kept courts.

Besides these in particular, both the earls and king's thanes, together with the bishops, abbots, and vavasors of middle thanes, had in the high court or parliament of the kingdom a more public jurisdiction, consisting, first, of deliberative power for advising upon and assenting onto new laws, secondly; of giving counsel in matters of state; and thirdly, of judicature upon suits and complaints. I shall not omit to enlighten the obscurity of these times, in which there is little to be found of a methodical constitution of this high court, by the addition of an argument which I conceive to bear a strong testimony unto itself, though taken out of a late writing that conceals the author.

It is well known (saith he) /John Streater(?)/ that in every quarter of the realm a great many boroughs do yet send burgesses unto the parliament, which nevertheless be so anciently and so long since decayed and gone to naught, that they cannot be shown to have been of any reputation since the Conquest, much less to have obtained any such privilege by the grant of any succeeding king; wherefore these must have had this right by more ancient usage, and before the Conquest; they being unable now to show whence they derive it.

This argument (though there be more) I shall pitch upon as sufficient to prove, first, that the lower sort of the people had right unto session in parliament during the time of the Teutons /Saxons/. Secondly, that they were qualified unto the same by election in their boroughs and, if knights of the shire (as no doubt they are) be as ancient, in the counties. Thirdly, if it be a good argument to say that the commons during the reign of the Teutons were elected into parliament, because they are so now and no man can show when this custom began, I see not which way it should be an ill one to say that the commons during the reign of the Teutons /Saxons/ constituted also a distinct house, because they do so now, unless any man can show that they did ever sit in the same house with the lords. Wherefore, to conclude this part, I conceive, for these and other reasons to be mentioned hereafter, that the parliament of the Teutons /Saxons/ consisted of the king, the lords spiritual and temporal, and the commons of the nation, notwithstanding the style of divers acts of parliament which runs, as that of Magna Carta, in the king's name only, seeing the same was nevertheless enacted by the king, peers and commons of the land, as it testified in those words by a subsequent act.*

*Contrary to Harrington's assertion, parliament did not exist in the Anglo-Saxon period (560-1066).

The monarchy of the Teutons /Saxons/ had stood in this posture about two hundred and twenty years, when Turbo /William/, Duke of Neustria /Normandy/, making his claim to the crown of one of their kings that died childless, followed it with successful arms and, being possessed of the kingdom, used it as conquered, distributing the earldoms, thane-lands, bishoprics and prelacies of the whole realm amongst his Neustrians /Normans/. From this time the earl came to be called comes, consul and dux (though consul and dux grew afterward out of use). The king's thanes came to be called barons and their lands baronies; the middle thane, holding still of a mesne lord, retained the name of vivasor.

The earl or comes continued to have the third part of the pleas of the county paid unto him by the sheriff or vice-comes, now a distinct office in every county depending upon the king, saving that such earls as had their counties to their own use were now counts palatine, and had under the king regal jurisdiction, insomuch that they constituted their own sheriffs, granted pardons, and issued writs in their own names; nor did king's writ of ordinary justice run in their dominions, till a late statute whereby much of this privilege was taken away.

For barons, they came from henceforth to be in different times of three kinds; barons by their estates and tenures, barons by writ, and barons created by letters patents. From Turbo /William/ the first to Adoxus /John/ the seventh king from the conquest, barons had their denomination from their possessions and tenures, and these were either spiritual or temporal; for not only the thane-lands, but the possessions of bishops, as also of some twenty-six abbots and two priors, were now erected into baronies, whence the lords spiritual, that had suffrage in the Teuton /Saxon/ parliament as spiritual lords, came to have it in the Neustrian /Norman/ parliament as barons, and were made subject (which they had not formerly been) unto knight's service in chief. Barony coming henceforth to signify all honorary possessions, as well of earls as barons, and baronage to denote all kinds of lords, as well spiritual as temporal, having right to sit in parliament, the baronies in this sense were sometimes more and sometimes fewer, but commonly about two hundred or two hundred fifty, containing in them a matter of sixty thousand feuda militum, or knights' fees, whereof

some twenty-eight thousand were in the clergy. It is
ill luck that no man can tell what the land of a
knight's fee (reckoned in some writs as 40£ a year,
and in others as 10) was certainly worth, for by such
an help we might have exactly demonstrated the balance
of this government. But says /Sir Edward/ Coke*, it
contained twelve plough-lands, and that was thought
to be the most certain account; but this again is ex-
tremely uncertain, for one plough out of some land that
was fruitful might work more than ten out of some other
that was barren. Nevertheless, seeing it appeareth
by /Henry/ Bracton+ that of earldoms and baronies it
was wont to be said that the whole kingdom was composed,
as also that these, consisting of 60,000 knight's fees,
furnished 60,000 men for the king's service (being the
whole militia of this monarchy), it cannot be imagined
that the vavasories or freeholds in the people amounted
to any considerable proportion. Wherefore the balance
and foundation of this government was in the 60,000
knight's fees and, these being possessed by the two
hundred and fifty lords, it was a government of the
few, or of the nobility, wherein the people also assemble, but could have no more than a mere name. And
the clergy holding a third of the whole nation, as is
plain by the parliament roll, it is an absurdity -
seeing the clergy of France came first through their
riches to be a state of that kingdom - to acknowledge
the people to have been a state of this realm and not
to allow it unto the clergy, who were so much more
weighty in the balance, which is that of all other
whence a state or order in a government is denominated;
wherefore this monarchy consisted of the king and of
the three ordines regni or estates: the lords spiritual
and temporal, and the commons. It consisted of these,
I say, as to the balance, though during the reign of
some of these kings not as to the administration.

For the ambition of Turbo /William/, and some of
those that more immediately succeeded him, to be absolute princes, strove against the nature of their
foundation and, inasmuch as he had divided almost the
whole realm among his Neustrians /Normans/, with some
encouragement for a while. But the Neustrians - while
they were but foreign plants, having no security against
the natives but in growing up by their prince's sides -
were no sooner well rooted in their vast dominions than

*Author of Institutes, d. 1634.
+Author of Treatise on Law, d. 1268.

they came up according to the infallible consequences
of the balance domestic and, contracting the national
interest of the baronage, grew as fierce in the vindication of the ancient rights and liberties of the same
as if they had been always natives; whence, the kings
being as obstinate on the one side for their absolute
power as these on the other for their immunities, grew
certain wars which took their denomination from the
barons.

    This fire about the middle of the reign of Adoxus
/John/ began to break out; and whereas the predecessors
of this king had diverse times been forced to summon
councils resembling those of the Teutons /Saxons/,
unto which the lords only that were barons by dominion
and tenure had hitherto repaired, Adoxus /John/, seeing
the effects of such dominion, began first, not to call
such as were barons by writs, for that was according
to the practice of ancient times, but to call such by
writs as were otherwise no barons, by which means,
striving to avoid the consequence of the balance, in
coming unwillingly to set the government straight, he
was the first that set it awry. For the barons in his
reign and his successor's, having vindicated their
ancient authority, restored the parliament with all the
rights and privileges of the same, saving that from
thenceforth the kings had found out a way whereby to
help themselves against the mighty; creatures of their
own, and such as had no other support by by their
favour. By which means this government, being indeed
the masterpiece of modern prudence, hath been cried
up to the skies as the only invention whereby at once
to maintain the sovereignty of a prince and the liberty
of the people; whereas indeed it hath been no other
than a wrestling match, wherein the nobility, as they
have been stronger, have thrown the king, or the king,
if he have been stronger, hath thrown the nobility; or
the king, where he hath had a nobility and could bring
them to his party, hath thrown the people, as in France
and Spain; or the people, where they have had no nobility, or could get them to be of their party, have
thrown the king, as in Holland and of latter times in
Oceana /England/. But they came not to this strength
but by such approaches and degrees, as remain to be
further opened. For whereas the barons by writs (as
the sixty-four abbots and thirty-six priors that were
so called) were but pro tempore, Dicotome /Richard II/,
being the twelfth king from the conquest, began to make
barons by letters patent, with the addition of honorary

pensions for the maintenance of their dignities to them
and their heirs; so that they were hands in the king's
purse, and had no shoulders for his throne. Of these
when the house of peers came once to be full, as will
be seen hereafter, there was nothing more empty. But
for the present, the throne having other supports, they
did not hurt that so much as they did the king; for the
old barons, taking Dicotome's /Richard II/ prodigality
to such creatures so ill that they deposed him, got the
trick of it, and never gave over setting up and pulling
down of their kings, according to their various interests and that faction of the white and red into which
they had been thenceforth divided, till Panurgus
/Henry VII/, the eighteenth king from the conquest,
was more by their favour than his right advanced unto
the crown.

TUDOR ENGLAND

This king /Henry VII/, through his natural subtle-
ty, reflecting at once upon the greatness of their
/Barons/ power and the inconstancy of thir favour,
began to find another flaw in this kind of government,
which is also noted by Machiavel /Machivelli, The
Prince/: namely, that a throne supported by a nobility
is not so hard to be ascended, as kept warm. Wherefore his secret jealousy lest the dissension of the
nobility, as it brought him in, might throw him out,
travelled in ways undiscovered by them unto ends as
little foreseen by himself, while to establish his own
safety he, by mixing water with their wine, first began
to open those sluices that have since overwhelmed not
the king only, but the throne; for whereas a nobility
striketh not at the throne, without which they cannot
subsist, but at some king that they do not like, popular power striketh through the king at the throne, as
that which is incompatible with it. Now that Panurgus
/Henry VII/, in abating the power of the nobility, was
the cause whence it came to fall into the hands of the
people, appears by those several statutes that were
made in his reign; as that for population, those against
retainers, and that for alienations.

By the statute of population /1489/, all houses of
husbandry that were used with twenty acres of ground
and upwards were to be maintained and kept up for ever,
with a competent proportion of land laid to them and in
no wise, as appears by a subsequent statute, to be

severed. By which means the houses being kept up, did of necessity enforce dwellers; and the proportion of land to be tilled being kept up, did of necessity enforce the dweller not to be a beggar or cottager, but a man of some substance, that might keep friends and servants and set the plough on going. This did mightily concern (saith the historian of that prince)* the might and manhood of the kingdom, and in effect amortize a great part of the lands unto the hold and possession of the yoemanry, or middle people, who, living not in a servile or indigent fashion, were much unlinked from dependence upon their lords and, living in a free and plentiful manner, become a more excellent infantry, but such an one upon which the lords had so little power, that from henceforth they may be computed to have been disarmed.

And as they lost their infantry after this manner, so their cavalry and commanders were cut off by the statute of retainers /1504/; for whereas it was the custom of the nobility to have younger brothers of good houses, mettled fellows and such as were knowing in the feats of arms, about them, they who were longer followed with so dangerous a train escaped not such punishment as made them take up.

Henceforth the country lives and great tables of the nobility which no longer nourished veins that would bleed for them, were fruitless and loathsome till they changed the air, and of princes became courtiers, where their revenues, never to have been exhausted by beef and mutton, were found narrow; whence followed rackings of rents and at length sale of lands, the riddance through the statute of alienations being rendered far more quick and facile than formerly it had been, by the new invention of entails.

To this it happened that Coraunus /Henry VIII/, the successor of that king, dissolving the abbeys, brought with the declining estate of the nobility so vast a prey unto the industry of the people, that the balance of the commonwealth was too apparently in the popular party to be unseen by the wise council of Queen Parthenia /Elizabeth/ who, converting her reign through the perpetual love tricks that passed between her and her people into a kind of romance, wholly neglected the nobility. And by these degrees came the house of commons to raise that head, which since hath been so

*Francis Bacon, History of King Henry VII (1622).

high and formidable unto their princes that they have looked pale upon those assemblies. Nor was there anything now wanting unto the destruction of the throne but that the people, not apt to see their own strength, should be put to feel it, when a prince /Charles/, as stiff in disputes as the nerve of monarchy was grown slack, received that unhappy encouragement from his clergy which became his utter ruin; while, trusting more unto their logic than the rough philosophy of his parliament, it came unto an irreparable breach; for the house of peers /Lords/, which alone had stood in this gap, now sinking down between the king and the commons, showed that Crassus* was dead and Isthmus broken. But a monarchy divested of her nobility hath no refuge under heaven but an army. <u>Wherefore the dissolution of this government caused the war, not the war the dissolution of this government.</u>

Of the king's /Charles I/ success with his arms it is not necessary to give any further account, than that they proved as ineffectual as his nobility. But without a nobility or an army (as hath been shown) there can be no monarchy. Wherefore what is there in nature that can arise out of these ashes but a popular government, or a new monarchy to be erected by the victorious army?

To erect a monarchy, be it ever so new, unless like Leviathan+ you can hang it (as the country fellow speaks) by geometry (for what else is it to say that every other man must give up his will unto the will of this one man without any other foundation?), it must stand upon old principles, that is upon nobility or an army planted upon a due balance of dominion. <u>Aut viam inveniam aut faciam</u> was an adage of Caesar's; and there is no standing for a monarchy unless she finds this balance or make it. If she find it, her work's done unto her hand; for where there is inequality of estates, there must be inequality of power, and where there is inequality of power, there can be no commonwealth. To make it, her sword must extripate out of dominion all other roots of power, and plant her army upon that ground. An army may be planted nationally or provincially. To plant it nationally, it must be in one of the four ways mentioned: that is, either monarchically in part, as the Roman <u>beneficiarii</u>; or monarchically in the whole, as the Turkish timariots; aristocratical-

---

*Member of Rome's first Triumvirate.
+Title of Thomas Hobbes' book, 1651.

ly, that is, by earls and barons, as the Neustrians /Normans/ were planted by Turbo /William/; or democratically, that is by equal lots, as the Israelitish army in the land of Canaan by Joshua. In every one of these ways there must not only be confiscations, but confiscations unto such a proportion as may answer to the work intended.

SEVENTEENTH CENTURY ENGLAND

To come then to the generation of the commonwealth, it hath been shown how, through the ways and means used by Panurgus /Henry VII/ to abase the nobility, and so to mend the flaw which we have asserted to be incurable in this kind of constitution, he suffered the balance to fall into the power of the people and so broke the government; but the balance being in the people, the commonwealth (though they do not see it) is already in the nature of them. <u>Cornua nota prius vitulo quam frontibus extant</u>. There wanteth nothing else but time (which is slow and dangerous) or art (which would be more quick and secure) for the bringing those native arms - wherewithal they are found already to resist, they know not how, everything that opposeth them - unto such maturity as may fix them upon their own strength and bottom.

But whereas this art is prudence /learning/, and that part of prudence which regards the present work is nothing else but the skill of raising such superstructures of government as are natural to the known foundations, they never mind the foundation but, through certain animosities (wherewith by striving one against another they are infected), or through certain freaks by which, not regarding the course of things nor how they conduce unto their purpose, they are given to building in the air, come to be divided and subdivided into endless parties and factions, both civil and ecclesiastical; which briefly to open, I shall first speak of the people in general, and then of their divisions.

A people (saith Machiavel /Machiavelli/) that is corrupt is not capable of a commonwealth; but in showing what a corrupt people is, he hath either involved himself or me, nor can I otherwise come out of the labyrinth than by saying that, the balance altering, a people, as to the foregoing government, must of necessity be corrupt; but corruption in this sense signifieth no more than that the corruption of one government (as in natural bodies) is the generation of another; wherefore, if the balance alter from monarchy, the corruption of the people in this case is that which maketh them capable of a commonwealth. But whereas I am not ignorant that the corruption which he meaneth is in manners, this also is from the balance. For the balance, swaying from monarchical into popular, abateth the luxury of the nobility and, enriching the people, bringeth the government from a more private unto a more public interest, which, coming nearer, as hath been shown, unto justice and right reason, the people upon a like alteration is so far from such corruption of manners as should render them incapable of a commonwealth, that of necessity they must thereby contract such reformation of manners as will bear no other kind of government. On the other side, where the balance changeth from popular to oligarchical or monarchical, the public interest, with the reason and justice included in the same, becometh more private; luxury is introduced in the place of temperance and servitude in that of freedom, which causeth such a corruption of manners both in the nobility and the people as, by the example of Rome in the time of the Triumvirs, is more at large discovered by the author to have been altogether incapable of a commonwealth.

But the balance of Oceana /England/ changing quite contrary to that of Rome, the manners of the people were not thereby corrupted, but on the contrary fitted for a commonwealth. For differences of opinion in a people not rightly informed of their balance, or division into parties while there is not any common ligament of power sufficient to reconcile or hold them, is no sufficient proof of corruption in a people. Nevertheless, seeing this must needs be matter of scandal and danger, it will not be amiss, in showing what were the parties, to show what were their errors.

The parties into which this nation was divided were temporal or spiritual; and the temporal parties were especially two, the one the royalists, the other commonwealthsmen, each of which asserted their different causes, either out of prudence /learning/ or ignorance, out of interest or conscience.

For prudence /learning/, either that of the ancients is inferior unto the modern (which we have hitherto been setting face to face, that any one may judge), or that of the royalists must be inferior unto that prudence of the commonwealthsman; and for interest, taking the commonwealthsman to have really intended the public (for otherwise he is an hypocrite, and the worst of men), that of the royalist must of necessity have been more private; wherefore the whole dispute will come upon matter of conscience, and this, whether it be urged by the right of kings, the obligation of former laws, or of the oath of allegiance, is absolved by the balance.

For if the right of kings were as immediately derived from the breath of God as the life of man, yet this excludeth not death and dissolution. But that the dissolution of the late monarchy was as natural as the death of a man hath been already shown; wherefore it remains with the royalists to discover by what reason of experience it is possible for a monarchy to stand upon a popular balance; or, the balance being popular, as well the oath of allegiance as all other monarchical laws imply an impossibility, and are therefore void.

To the commonwealthsman I have no more to say but that if he exclude any party, he is not truly such, or shall ever found a commonwealth upon the natural principle of the same, which is justice; and the royalist, for having opposed a commonwealth in Oceana /England/ (where the laws were so ambiguous that they might be eternally disputed and never reconciled), can neither be justly for that cause excluded from his full and equal share in the government, nor prudently for this, that a commonwealth consisting of a party will be in perpetual labour of her own destruction; whence it was that the Romans, having conquered the Albans /English/, incorporated them with equal right into the commonwealth, and if the royalists be flesh of your flesh, and nearer of blood than were the Albans to the Romans, you are also Christians. Nevertheless there is no reason that a commonwealth should any more favour a party remaining in fixed opposition against her than Brutus did his sons. But if she fix them upon that opposition, it is her fault, not theirs, and this is done by excluding them. Men that have equal possessions and the same security of their estates and of their liberties that you have, have the same cause with you to defend; but if you will be trampling, they fight for liberty, though for monarchy, and you for tyranny, though under the name of a commonwealth; the nature of orders in a commonwealth rightly instituted being void of all jealousy, because, let the parties which she embraceth be what they will, her orders are such as they neither would resist if they could, nor could if they would, as hath in part been already shown, and will appear more at large by the ensuing model.

The parties that are spiritual are of more kinds than I need mention: some for a national religion and other for liberty of conscience, with such animosity on both sides as if these two did not consist; of which I have already sufficiently spoken to show that the one cannot well consist without the other. But they of all the rest are the most dangerous who, holding that the saints must govern, go about to reduce the commonwealth unto a party; as well for the reasons already shown, as that their pretenses are against Scripture, where the saints are commended to submit unto the higher powers, and be subject unto the ordinance of man. And that men pretending under the notion of saints or religion unto civil power have hitherto never failed to dishonour that profession, the world is full of examples, whereof I shall confine myself at the present unto two, the one of old, the other of new Rome.

In old Rome the patricians or nobility, pretending to be the godly party, were questioned by the people for engrossing all the magistracies of that commonwealth, and had nothing to say why they did so, but <u>quod nemo plebeius auspicia haberet</u>; that magistracy required a kind of holiness which was not in the people. <u>Plebs ad id maxima indignatione exarsit, quod auspicari tanquam invisi diis immortalibus negarentur posse</u>; at which the people were filled with such indignation as had come to cutting of throats, if the nobility had not forthwith laid by the insolency of that plea, which nevertheless when they had done, the people for a long time after continued to elect none other than patrician magistrates.

The example of new Rome in the rise and practice of the hierarchy (too well known to require any further illustration) is far more immodest.

This hath been the course of nature; and when it hath pleased or shall please God to introduce anything that is above the course of nature, he will, as he hath always done, confirm it by miracle; for so in his prophecy of the reign of Christ upon earth, he expressly promiseth, seeing that the souls of them that were beheaded for Jesus shall be seen to live and reign with him, which will be an object of sense; the rather because the rest of the dead are not to live again until the thousand years be finished. And it is not lawful for men to persuade us that a thing is, though there be no such object of our sense, which God hath told us shall not be until it be an object of our sense.

The saintship of a people as to government consisteth in the election of magistrates fearing God and hating covetousness, and not in their confining themselves or being confined unto men of this or that party or profession. It consisteth in making the most prudent and religious choice that they can, but not in trusting unto men but, next God, in their orders. 'Give us good men and they will make us good laws' is the maxim of a demagogue, and (through the alteration which is commonly perceivable in men, when they have power to work their own wills) exceeding fallible. But 'give us good orders, and they will make us good men' is the maxim of a legislator and the most infallible in the politics.

But these divisions (however there be some good men that look sadly on them) are trivial things: first (as to the civil concernment), because the government whereof this nation is capable, once seen, taketh in all interests. And secondly (as to the spiritual) because, as pretence of religion hath always been turbulent in broken government, so where the government hath been sound and steady, religion hath never shown herself with any other face than that of her natural sweetness and tranquility, nor is there any reason why she should; wherefore the errors of the people are occasioned by their governors. If they be doubtful of the way or wander from it, it is because their guides misled them; and the guides of the people are never so well qualified for leading by any virtue of their own, as by that of the government.

The government of Oceana /England/ (as it stood at the time whereof we discourse) consisting of one single council of the people, to the exclusion of the king and of the lords, was called a parliament; howbeit the parliaments of the Teutons /Saxons/ and of the Neustrians /Normans/ consisted, as hath been shown, of the king, lords and commons, wherefore this under an old name was a new thing: a parliament consisting of a single assembly, elected by the people and invested with the whole power of government, without any covenants, conditions, or orders whatsoever. So new a thing that neither ancient nor modern prudence can show any avowed example of the like; and there is scarce anything that seemeth unto me so strange as that (whereas there was nothing more familiar with these counsellors than to bring the Scripture to the House) there should not be a man of them that so much as offered to bring the House unto the Scripture, wherein, as hath been shown, it contained that original whereof all the rest of the commonwealths seem to be copies. Certainly if Leviathan /Thomas Hobbes/ (who is surer of nothing than that a popular commonwealth consisteth but of one council) transcribed his doctrine out of this assembly, for him to except against Aristotle and Cicero for writing out of their own commonwealths was not so fair play; or if the parliament transcribed out of him, it had been an honour better due unto Moses. But where one of them should have an example but from the other, I cannot imagine; there being nothing of this kind that I can find in story but the oligarchy of Athens, the thirty tyrants of the same, and the Roman decemvirs.

For the oligarchy, Thucydides* tells us that it was a senate or council of four hundred, pretending to a balancing council of the people consisting of five thousand, but not producing them; wherein you have the definition of an oligarchy, which is a single council both debating and resolving, dividing and choosing; and what that must come to was shown by the example of the girls, and is apparent through all experience. Wherefore the thirty set up by the Lacedaemonians when they had conquered Athens are called tyrants by all authors, Leviathan only excepted, who will have them against all the world to have been an aristocracy, but for what reason I cannot imagine, there also as void of any balance having been void of that which is essential to every commonwealth, whether aristocratical or popular; except he be pleased with them in that, by the testimony of Xenophon, they killed more men in eight months than the Lacedaemonians had done in ten years, oppressing the people (to use Sir Walter Ralegh's words) with all base and intolerable slavery.

The usurped government of the decemvirs in Rome was of the same kind. Wherefore in the fear of God let

*Green historian.

Christian legislators, setting the pattern given in the Mount on the one side, and these execrable examples on the other, know the right hand from the left, and so much the rather because those things which do not conduce to the good of the governed are fallacious if they appear to be good for the governors. God in chastising a people is accustomed to burn his rod. The empire of these oligarchies was not so violent as short, nor did they fall upon the people but in their own immediate ruin. A council without a balance is not a commonwealth, but an oligarchy; and every oligarchy, except she be put to the defence of her wickedness or power against some outward danger, is factious. Wherefore, the errors of the people being from their government (which maxim in the politics, bearing a sufficient testimony unto itself, is also proved by Machiavel), if the people of Oceana /England/ have been factious the cause is apparent. But what remedy?

In answer to this question, I come now to the army, of which the most victorious captain and incomparable patriot Olphaus Megaletor /Oliver Cromwell/ was now general who, being a much greater master of that art whereof I have made a rough draft in these preliminaries, had so sad reflections upon the ways and proceedings of the parliament as cast him upon books and all other means of diversion, among which he happened upon this place of Machiavel /Machiavelli/. 'Thrice happy is that people which chances to have a man able to give them such a government at once, as without alteration may secure them of their liberties; seeing it is certain that Lacedaemon, in observing the laws of Lycurgus, continued about eight hundred years without any dangerous tumult or corruption.' My lord general (as it is said of Themistocles that he could not sleep for the glory obtained by Miltiades at the battle of Marathon) took so new and deep impression at these words of the much greater glory of Lycurgus that, being on this side assaulted with the emulation of his illustrious object, on the other with the misery of the nation, which seemed (as it were ruined by his victory) to cast herself at his feet, he was also wholly deprived of his natural rest, until the debate he had within himself came to a firm resolution: that the greatest advantages of a commonwealth are, first, that the legislator should be one man, and secondly that the government should be made altogether, or at once. For the first, it is certain, said Machiavel, that a commonwealth is seldom or never well turned or constituted, except it have been the work of one man; for which cause a wise legislator, and one whose mind is firmly set not upon private but the public interest, not upon his posterity but upon his country, may justly endeavour to get the sovereign power into his own hands, nor shall any man that is master of reason blame such extraordinary means as in that case shall be necessary, the end proving no other than the constitution of a well-ordered commonwealth. The reason of this is demonstrable; for the ordinary means not failing, the commonwealth hath no need of a legislator, but the ordinary means failing, there is no recourse to be had but to such as are extraordinary. And whereas a book or a building hath not been known to attain perfection, if it had not had a sole author or architect, a commonwealth, as to the fabric of it, is of the like nature. And thus it may be made at once, in which there be great advantages: for a commonwealth made at once taketh her security at the same time she lendeth her money, trusteth not herself to the faith of men but launcheth immediately forth into the empire of laws and, being set straight, bringeth the manners of her citizens unto her rule; whence followed that uprightness which was in Lacedaemon. But manners that are rooted in men bow the tenderness of a commonwealth, coming up by twigs unto their bent; whence followed the obliquity that was in Rome, and those perpetual repairs by the counsuls' axes and tribunes' hammers, which could never finish that commonwealth but in destruction.

My lord general, being clear in these points and the necessity of some other course than would be thought upon by the parliament, appointed a rendezvous of the army, where he spoke his sense agreeable to these preliminaries, with such success unto the soldiery that the parliament was soon after deposed; and himself, in the great hall of the Pantheon or Palace of Justice situated in Emporium /London/ the capital city, created, by the universal suffrage of the army, Lord Archon, or sole legislator of Oceana /England/; upon which theatre you have, to conclude this piece, a person introduced whose fame shall never draw his curtain.

CHAPTER III

COMMONWEALTH OF OCEANA:

HARRINGTON'S CONSTITUTION FOR ENGLAND

"Commonwealths, of all other governments, are more especially for the preservation, not the destruction of mankind."

Aphorisms Political

The selections printed below outline Harrington's constitution for Oceana, his fictitious name for England. The selections are taken from the various writings of Harrington between 1654 and 1661. Most of the information can be found in any one of the writings, and the constitution in its original and most complete form is in The Commonwealth of Oceana. All the later essays are explanations of Oceana. Rather than reproducing Oceana, the editor has chosen from the various writings of Harrington what he believes to be the most lucid and most comprehensible explanation of that part of the constitution. The particular source of each selection will be noted at the end of that section. Ellipses indicate omitted paragraphs of the same source.

The only part of Harrington's constitution for England that has been purposely ignored is the one dealing with the provinces - Scotland and Ireland. Harrington was an imperialist, wanting to keep Scotland and Ireland as subordinate colonies of England. He had to violate the highest principles in his constitution in order to do this. Therefore the editor has included this part of the constitution only in the summary section at the end.

The institutions of government have been arranged in the order that Harrington usually arranged them in his writings. A quick look at the Table of Contents or the Diagram of Government at the end of the book will give one the outline of his government institutions.

The last selection in this section is The Rota. It was the last actual outline of his constitution that Harrington wrote, and it may be the best short summary of the constitution.

COMMONWEALTH

The definition /for commonwealth/ is contained in the first of my preliminaries, which because it is short I shall repeat.

'An equal commonwealth is a government established upon an equal agrarian arising into the superstructures or three orders: the senate debating and proposing, the people resolving, and the magistracy executing, by an equal rotation or interchangeable election, through the suffrage of the people given by the ballot.' The exemplification is the whole commonwealth of Oceana.*

If the whole people be landlords, or hold the lands so divided among them, that no one man, or number of men, within the compass of the few or aristocracy, overbalance them, the empire (without the interposition of force) is a commonwealth.

. . . .

An equal commonwealth is such as one as is equal in the balance or foundation and in the superstructures, that is to say in her agrarian law and in her rotation.

An equal agrarian is a perpetual law establishing and preserving the balance of dominion, by such a distribution of land that no one man or number of men within the compass of the few or aristocracy can come to overpower the whole people by their possessions in lands.

As the agrarian answereth unto the foundation, so doth rotation unto the superstructures.

Equal rotation is equal vicissitude in government, or succession unto magistracy conferred for such convenient terms, enjoying equal vacations, as take in the whole body by parts, succeeding others through the free election or suffrage of the people.

. . . .

An equal commonwealth (by that which hath been said) is a government established upon an equal agrarian, arising into the superstructures or three orders, the

*The Prerogative of Popular Government.

senate debating and proposing, the people resolving, and the magistracy executing by an equal rotation through the suffrage of the people given by the ballot. For though rotation may be without the ballot, and the ballot without rotation, yet the ballot not only as to the ensuing model includeth both, but is by far the most equal way; for which cause under the name of the ballot I shall hereafter understand both that and rotation too.

Now, having reasoned the principles of an equal commonwealth, I should come to give an instance of such an one in experience, if I could find it; but if this work be of any value, it lieth in that it is the first example of a commonwealth that is perfectly equal. For Venice, though she come the nearest, yet is a commonwealth for preservation; and such an one, considering the paucity of citizens taken in, and the number not taken in, is externally unequal; and though every commonwealth that holdeth provinces must in that regard be such, yet not unto that degree. Nevertheless Venice internally and for her capacity is by far the most equal.*

Where the people are not over-balanced by one man or by the few, they are not capable of any other superstructures of government, or of any other just and quiet settlement whatsoever, that of such as consisteth of a senate as their counsellors, of themselves or their representatives as sovereign lords, and of a magistracy unswerable unto the people as distributors and executioners of the laws made by the people; and thus much is of absolute necessity unto any or every government that is or can properly be called a commonwealth, whether it be well or ill ordered.

But the necessary definition of a commonwealth anything well ordered is that it is a government consisting of the senate proposing, the people resolving, and the magistracy executing.+

AGRARIAN LAW

Property is that which is every man's own by the law of the land, and of this there is nothing stirred, but all entirely left as it was found, by the agrarian of Oceana.

*The Commonwealth of Oceana.
+The Arts of Lawgiving.

Property in money (except, as hath been shown, in cities that have little or no territory) cometh not unto the present account. But property in land, according to the distribution that happeneth to be of the same, causeth the political balance producing empire of the like nature; that is, if the property in lands be so diffused through the whole people that neither one landlord nor a few landlords over-balance them, the empire is popular. If the property in lands be so engrossed by the few that they over-balance the whole people, the empire is aristocratical or mixed monarchy; but if property in lands be in one landlord, to such a proportion as over-balanceth the whole people, the empire is absolute monarchy. So the political balance is three-fold, democratical, aristocratical, and monarchical.

Each of these balances may be introduced either by the legislator at the institution of the government, or by civil vicissitude, alienation or alteration of property under government.

Examples of the balance introduced at the institution and by the legislator are, first, those in Israel and Lacedaemon, introduced by God, or Moses, and Lycurgus, which were democratical or popular. Secondly, those in England, France and Spain, introduced by the Goths, Vandals, Saxons and Franks, which were aristocratical, or such as produced the government of king, lords and commons. Thirdly, those in the east and Turkey, introduced by Nimrod and Mahomet or Ottoman, which were purely monarchical.

Examples of the balance introduced by civil vicissitude, alienation or alteration of property under government are: in Florence where, the Medici attaining to excessive wealth, the balance altered from popular to monarchical. In Greece, where 'the Argives being lovers of equality and liberty, reduced the power of their kings to so small a matter, that there remained unto the children and successors of Cisus, little more than the title'; where the balance altered from monarchical to popular. In Rome, about the time of Crassus, the nobility having eaten the people out of their lands, the balance altered from popular first unto aristocratical, as in the triumvirs, Caesar, Pompey and Crassus, and then to monarchical, as when, Crassus being dead and Pompey conquered, the whole came to Caesar. 'In Tarentum, not long after the war with the Medes, the nobility being wasted and overcome by the Iapyges, the balance, and with that the commonwealth, changed from aristocratical to popular'; the like of late hath discovered itself in Oceana. When a balance cometh so through civil vicissitude to be changed, that the change cannot be attributed unto human providence, it is more peculiarly to be ascribed unto the hand of God; and so when there happeneth to be an irrestible change of the balance, not the old government which God repealed, but the new government, which he dictateth as present legislator, is of divine right.

This volubility of the balance being apparent, it belongs unto legislators to have eyes, and to occur with some prudential or legal remedy or prevention; and the laws that are made in this case are called agrarian. So an agrarian is a law fixing the balance of a government, in such manner that it cannot alter.

This may be done divers ways, as by entailing the lands upon certain families, without power of alienation in any case, as in Israel and Lacedaemon, or except with leave of the magistrate, as in Spain; but this, by making some families too secure, as those in possession, and other too dispairing, as those not in possession, may make the whole people less industrious.

Wherefore the other way, which by the regulation of purchases ordains only that a man's land shall not exceed some certain proportions - for example, two thousand pounds a year; or, exceeding such a proportion, shall divide in descending unto the children, so soon as, being more than one, they shall be capable of such division or sub-division, till the greater share exceed not two thousand pounds a year in land, lying and being within the native territory - is that which is received and established by the commonwealth of Oceana.*

Fixation of the balance of property is not to be provided for but by laws; and the laws whereby such provision is made are commonly called agrarian laws. Now as governments through the diverse balance of property are of diverse or contrary natures, that is monarchical or popular; so are such laws. Monarchy requires of the standard of property that it be vast or great; and of agrarian laws that they bar recess or

*The Prerogative of Popular Government.

diminution, at least insomuch as is thereby entailed upon the honour. But popular government requires that her standard be moderate, and that her agrarian bar accumulation. In a territory not exceeding England in revenue, if the balance be in more hands than three hundred, it is upon swaying from monarchy; and if it be in fewer than five thousand hands, it is swaying from a commonwealth; which as to this point may suffice at present.*

As to instance yet farther in that which is proposed by the present order to this nation, the standard whereof is at two thousand prounds a year: the whole territory of Oceana, being divided by this proportion, amounteth unto five thousand lots. So the lands of Oceana, being thus distributed, and bound unto this distribution, can never fall unto fewer than five thousand proprietors. But five thousand proprietors so seised will not agree to break the agrarian, for that were to agree to rob one another; nor to bring in a king, because they must maintain him and can have no benefit by him; nor to exclude the people, because they can have as little by that, and must spoil their militia. So the commonwealth, continuing upon the balance proposed, though it should come into five thousand hands, can never alter; and that it should ever come into five thousand hands, is as improbable as anything in the world that is not altogether impossible.+

Seeing it hath been sufficiently proved that empire followeth the nature of property, that the kind of empire or government dependeth upon the kind of distribution (except in small countries) of land, and that where the balance in property hath not been fixed, the kind of nature of the government hath been floating; it is good reason that, in the proposition of a commonwealth, we begin with fixation of the balance in property and, this being no otherwise to be done than by some such laws as have been commonly called agrarian, it is proposed:

1. That everyone holding above two thousand pounds a year in land, lying within the proper territory of the commonwealth, leave the said land equally divided among his sons; or else

*The Art of Lawgiving.
+The Commonwealth of Oceana.

so near equally that there remain unto the eldest of them not above two thousand pounds a year in land so lying. That this proposition be so understood as not to concern any parent having no more than one son, but the next heir only that shall have more sons; in such short as nothing be hereby taken from any man, or from his posterity, but that fatherly affection be at all points attended as formerly, save only that it be with more piety and less partiality. And that the same proposition, in such families where there are no sons, concern the daughters in like manner.

2. That no daughter, being neither heir nor co-heir, have above fifteen hundred pounds in portion, or for her preferment in marriage. That any daughter, being an orphan, and having seven hundred pounds or upward in portion, may charge the state with it. That the state, being so charged, be bound to manage the portion of such orphan for the best, either by due payment of the interest of the same; or if it be desired, by way of annuity for life, at the rate of one hundred pounds a year for every seven hundred pounds so received.

. . . .

That no agrarian law hereby given to this commonwealth, or be hereafter given unto the same, or any province of the same, be understood to be otherwise binding than to the generation to come, or to the children to be born seven years after the enacting of the law.

Upon the addition of this clause, it may be safely said of these agrarian laws that they concern not any man living; and for posterity, it is well known that to enact a law is no more in their regard than to commend a thing to their choice, seeing they, having the will, can no more be divested of the power to repeal any law enacted by their ancestors than we are of repealing such laws as have been enacted by ours.

To this it may be objected that agrarian laws, being once enacted, must have brought estates unto the standard of the same, before posterity can come into the capacity to judge of them. But this is the only means whereby posterity can come unto a true capacity to judge of them: first, because they will have had experience of the laws which they are to judge of; and secondly, because they will be void of all such imaginary interests as might corrupt their judgment, and do now certainly corrupt ours.*

Wherefore neither doth the agrarian proposed, taking the balance of estates as she now findeth them, 'make war against', but confirm the present customs. The only objection that can seem in this place to lie is that, whereas it hath been the custom of Oceana that the bulk of the estate should descend unto the eldest son, by the agrarian he cannot, in case he have more brothers, inherit above two thousand pounds a year in land, or an equal share. But neither doth this, whether you regard the parents or the children, make war with custom. For putting the case the father have twenty thousand pounds a year in land, he goes not the less in his custom or way of life for the agrarian, because for this he hath no less; and if he have more or fewer sons to whom this estate descends by equal or unequal portions, neither do they go less in their ways or customs of life for the agrarian, because they never had more. But, says Aristotle (speaking of the ostracism as it supplies the defect of an agrarian), 'this course is as necessary unto kings, as unto commonwealths'. By this means the monarchies of Turkey and of Spain preserve their balance; through the neglect of this hath that of the nobility of Oceana been broken; and this is it which the Prevaricator, in advising that the nobility be no farther levelled than will serve to keep the people under, requires of his prince. So, that an agrarian is necessary to government, be it what it will, is on all hand concluded.

. . . .

I have spoken of the many and, in speaking of the many, implicitly of the few; for as in an unequal commonwealth, for example England during the peerage or aristocracy, the many depended upon or were included in the few, so in an equal commonwealth the few depend upon or are included in the many, as the senate of Venice depends upon or is included in the great council, by which it is annually elected in the whole or in some part. So what was said in an equal commonwealth of the many, or the poorer sort, is also said of the few, or

*The Art of Lawgiving.

of the richer, who, through the virtue of the agrarian, as in Oceana, or of other orders supplying the defect of an agrarian, as in Venice, not able to overbalance the people, can never have any power to disturb the commonwealth in case they had such power. For example, in Oceana, putting the case that the few were as powerful as it is possible they should be, that is, that the whole land were fallen into five thousand hands; the five thousand, excluding the people, could get no more riches by it, because they have the whole land already, no more liberty by it, because they were in perfect liberty before, nor any more power by it, because through the equality of the balance, or of their estates, they can be no more by themselves than an equal commonwealth, and that they were with the people; but would be much less, the power or commonwealth in which there be five thousand equals being not greater but much less than the power or commonwealth wherein the whole people are equal, because the power or effect of a greater people is proportionably greater than the power or effect of a lesser people, and the few by this means would get no more than to be the lesser people. So, the people being no bar unto the riches, liberty nor power of the five thousand, and the desire of liberty, riches and power being the only causes of sedition, there could arise no sedition in this commonwealth by reason of the nobility, who have no such interest if they had the power, nor have any such power if they had the interest, the people being equally possessed of the government, of the arms, and far superior in number. In sum, an equal commonwealth consisteth but of one hereditary order, as the people, which is by election divided into two orders, as the senate and the congregation in Lacedaemon, or the senate and the great council in Venice; for the gentlemen of Venice, as hath been often said, are the people of Venice, the rest are subjects. And an unequal commonwealth consisteth of two hereditary orders, as the patricians and plebeians in Rome, whereof the former only had an hereditary capacity of the senate; whence it comes to pass that the senate and the people in an equal commonwealth having but one and the same interest, never were nor can be at variance, and that the senate and the people in an unequal commonwealth, having two distinct interests, never did nor can agree. So an equal commonwealth cannot be seditious, and an unequal commonwealth can be no other than seditious.*

*The Prerogative of Popular Government.

ROTATION

Rotation in a commonwealth is of the magistracy, of the senate, of the people, of the magistracy and the people, of the magistracy and the senate, or of the magistracy, the senate and the people; which in all come unto six kinds.

For example of rotation in the magistracy, you have the judge of Israel, called in Hebrew shophet. The like magistracy after the kings Ithobal and Baal came in use with the Tyrians; from these with their posterity the Carthaginians, who also called their supreme magistrates, being in number two and for their term annual, shophetim, which the Latins by a softer pronounciation render suffetes.

The shophet or judge of Israel was a magistrate, not, that I can find, obliged unto certain term, throughout the book of Judges; nevertheless, it is plain that his election was occasional and but for a time, after the manner of a dictator.

True it is that Eli and Samuel ruled all their lives, but upon this much impatience in the people followed, through the corruption of their sons, as was the main cause of the succeeding monarchy.

The magistrates in Athens (except the Aeropagites, being a judicatory) were all upon rotation. The like for Lacedaemon and Rome, except the kings in the former, who were indeed hereditary, but had no more power than the duke in Venice, where all the rest of the magistrates (except the procuratori, whose magistracy is but mere ornament) are also upon rotation.

For rotation of the senate you have Athens, the Achaeans, Aetolians, Lyceans, the Amphictionium, and the senate of Lacedaemon, reproved, in that it was for life, by Aristotle; modern examples of like kind are the diet of Switz, but especially the senate of Venice.

For the rotation of the people, you have first Israel, where the congregation, which the Greeks call ecclesia, the Latins comitia or concio - having a twofold capacity; first that of an army, in which they were the constant guard of the country; and secondly, that of a representative, in which they gave the vote of the people at the creation of their laws or election

of their magistrates - was monthly. Now the children
of Israel after their number, to wit, the chief fathers
and captains of thousands and hundreds, and their officers that served the king in any matter, of the courses which came in and went out month by month, throughout all the months of the year, every course, were
twenty and four thousand.*

Your galaxies, which divide the house into so many
regions, are three, one of which, constituting the third
region, is annually chosen, but for the term of three
years; which causeth the house, having blooms, fruit
half ripe, and others dropping off in full maturity, to
resemble an orange tree, such as is at the same time an
education or spring, and an harvest too. For the people
have made a very ill choice in the man who is not easily
capable of the perfect knowledge in one year of the senatorian orders; which knowledge, allowing him for the
first to have been a novice, brings him the second year
unto practice, and time enough; for at this rate you
must always have two hundred knowing men in the government, and thus the vicissitude of your senators is not
perceivable in the steadiness and perpetuity of your
senate, which, like that of Venice, being always changing, is forever the same. And though other politicians
have not so well imitated their pattern, there is nothing more obvious in nature, seeing a man, who wears the
same flesh but a short time, is nevertheless the same
man and of the same genius; and whence is this but from
the constancy of nature in holding a man unto her
orders? Wherefore hold also unto your orders. But
this is a mean request; your orders will be worth little
if they do not hold you unto them, wherefore embark.
They are like a ship; if you be once aboard, you do not
carry them but they you. And see how Venice stands unto
her tackling; you will no more forsake them than you
will leap into the sea.+

/One might argue/ that in a commonwealth
like that of Oceana, taking in the many . . . .,
where every man will press forward toward
magistracy, this law, by taking off at the
end of one year some officers, and all at the
end of three, will keep the republic in a
perpetual minority; no man having time allowed him to gain that experience which may

*The Prerogative of Popular Government.
+The Commonwealth of Oceana.

serve to lead the commonwealth to the understanding of her true interest either at home or abroad.

What I have confessed to be otherwise in Venice, I have shown already at least so far as concerneth the present occasion, the causes of that defect being incompatible with a commonwealth consisting of the many; otherwise why was not the like found in Athens or Rome, where though every man pressed forward towards magistracy, yet the magistrates were, for illustrious examples, more in weight and number than are to be found in all the rest of the world?

If where elections were the most exposed to the ambition of the competitor and the humours of the people, they yet failed not to excel all others that were not popular, what greater vindication can there be of the natural integrity of popular suffrage even at the worst? But this, where it is given by the ballot, is at the best, and free from all that pressing for magistracy in the competitor, or faction of the people, that can anyways be laid unto the former; or let the Considerer consider again, and tell me by what means either of these in such a state can be dangerous or troublesome, or if at worst the orders for election in Oceana must not perform that part better than a crowd and a sheriff. Well, but putting the case the elections, which were not quarrelled much withal, be rightly stated; yet this law for terms and vacations, 'by taking off at the end of one year some officers, and all at the end of three, will keep the republic in perpetual minority, no man having time allowed him to gain that experience which may serve to lead the commonwealth to the understanding of her true interest at home or abroad. Because 'every man will press forward for magistracy', therefore there ought not to be terms and vacations, lest these should 'keep the commonwealth in perpetual minority'. I would once see an argument that might be reduced to mood and figure. The next objection is that these orders 'take off at the end of one year some officers', which is true, and that 'at the end of three years, they take off all', which is false; for whereas the leaders of the commonwealth are all triennial, the orders every year take off no more than such only as have finished their three years' term, which is not all but a third part. Wherefore let him speak out: three years is too short a term for acquiring 'that knowledge, which is necessary unto the leading of a commonwealth'. To let the courses of Israel which were monthly, the annual magistracies of Athens and Rome go, if three years be too short a term for this purpose, what was three months, nor more frequent than once in a year, so that a man, having been twelve years a parliament man in England, could not have borne his magistracy above three years, though he were not necessarily subject unto any vacation; whereas a parliament man in Oceana may in twelve years have borne his magistracy six, notwithstanding the necessity of his vacations. Which of these two are the most straitened in the time necessary unto the gaining of experience or knowledge for the leading of a commonwealth? Nevertheless the parliament of England was seldom or never without men of sufficient skill and ability; though the orders there were more in number, less in method, not written and of greater difficulty than they be in Oceana. There, if not the parliament man, the parliament itself was upon terms and vacations, which unto a council of such nature is the most dangerous thing in the world, seeing dissolution, whether unto a body natural or political, is death. For if parliaments happened to rise again and again, this was not so much coming unto themselves (seeing a council of so different genius hath not been known) as a new birth, and a council that is every year new-born indeed must keep a commonwealth in perpetual minority or rather infancy, always in danger of being overlaid by her nurse or strangled by her guardian; whereas an assembly continued by succession or due rotation, regulated by terms, giving sufficient time for digestion, grows up and is like a man who, though he change his flesh, neither changeth his body nor his soul. Thus the senate of Venice, changing flesh, though not so often as in a commonwealth consisting of the many were requisite, yet oftenest of any other in the world, is, both in body and soul or genius, the most unchangeable council under heaven. Flesh must be changed or it will stink of itself; there is a term necessary to make a man able to lead the commonwealth unto her interest, and there is a term that may enable a man to lead the commonwealth unto his interest. In this regard it is, that (according to Mamercus) the vacations are <u>maxima libertatis custodia</u>, the keepers of the liberties of Oceana.

The three regions, into which each of the leading councils is divided, are three forms (as I may say) in the school of state. For them of the third (though there be care in the choice) it is no such great matter

what be their skill, the ballot, which they practiced
in the tribe, being that in the performance whereof no
man can be out, and this is all that is necessary unto
their novitiate or first year, during which time they
may be auditors; by the second they will have seen all
the scenes, of the whole rotation of the orders, so
facile and so intelligible that at one reading a man
understands them as a book but at one acting as a play,
and so methodical that he will remember them better.
Tell me then what it is that can hinder him for the
second year from being a speaker; or why, for the third,
should he not be a very able leader?

   The senate and the prerogative, or representative
of the people, being each of like constitution, drop
annually four hundred, which in a matter of ten years,
amount to four thousand experienced leaders, ready upon
new elections to resume their leading.*

LOCAL ADMINISTRATION

   The materials of a commonwealth are the people;
and the people of Oceana were distributed by casting
them into certain divisions, regarding their quality,
their ages, their wealth, and the places of their residence or habitation, which was done by the ensuing
orders.

>   The first distributing the people into free-
> men or citizens, and servants, while such;
> for if they attain unto liberty, that is to
> live of themselves, they are freemen or
> citizens.+

   The nature of riches considered, this division
(I say) into freemen and servants is not properly constitutive, but as it were natural. To come unto such
divisions as are both personal and constitutive, it is
proposed:

>   3. That all citizens, that is freemen, or
> such as are not servants, be distributed into
> horse and foot. That such of them as have
> one hundred pounds a year in lands, goods
> or money, or above that proportion, be of
> the horse; and all such as have under that
> proportion, be of the foot.

*The Prerogative of Popular Government.
+The Commonwealth of Oceana.

4. That all elders or freemen, being thirty years of age or upwards, be capable of civil administration; and that the youth, or such freemen as are between eighteen years of age and thirty, be not capable of civil administration, but of military only; in such manner as shall follow in the military part of this model.

Now besides personal divisions, it is, in order unto a commonwealth, of necessity that there be some such as are local. For these therefore it is proposed:

5. That the whole native or proper territory of the commonwealth be cast, with as much exactness as can be convenient, into known and fixed precincts or parishes.

6. That the elders resident in each parish annually assemble in the same; as for example, upon Monday next ensuing the last of December. That they then and there elect out of their own number every fifth man, or one man out of every five, to be for the term of the year ensuing a deputy of that parish; and that the first and second so elected be overseers or presidents, for the regulating of all parochial congregations, whether of the elders or of the youth, during the term for which they were elected.

7. That so many parishes lying nearest together, whose deputies shall amount to one hundred or thereabout, be cast into one precinct called the hundred. And that in each precinct called the hundred there be a town, village or place appointed to be the capital of the same.

8. That the parochial deputies elected throughout the hundred assemble annually, for example upon Monday next ensuing the last of January, at the capital of their hundred. That they then and there elect out of the horse of their number one justice of the peace, one juryman, one captain, one ensign; and out of the foot of their number, one other juryman, one high constable, etc.

Though our justices of peace have not been annual, yet that they may so be is apparent in that the high sheriffs, whose office is of greater difficulty, have always been annual; seeing therefore that they may be annual, that so they ought in this administration to be will appear, where they come to be constitutive of such courts as, should they consist of a standing magistracy, would be against the nature of a commonwealth. But the precincts hitherto being thus stated, it is proposed:

> 9. That every twenty hundred, lying nearest and most conveniently together, be cast into one tribe. That, the whole territory being after this manner cast into tribes, some town, village or place be appointed unto every tribe for the capital of the same. And that these three precincts, that is the parish, the hundred and the tribe, whether the deputies thenceforth annually chosen in the parishes or hundreds come to increase or diminish, remain firm and inalterable forever, save only by act of parliament.

These divisions, or the like both personal and local, are that in a well-ordered commonwealth which stairs are in a good house; not that stairs in themselves are desirable, but that without them there is no getting into the chambers. The whole matter of cost and pains required unto the introduction of a like model lieth only in the first architecture, or building of these stairs; that is, in stating of these three precincts; which done, they land you naturally and necessarily into all the rooms of this fabric. For the just number of tribes into which a territory thus cast may fall, it is not very easy to be guessed; yet because, for the carrying on of discourse, it is necessary to pitch upon some certainty, I shall presume that the number of the tribes thus stated amounts unto fifty; and that the number of the parochial deputies annually elected in each tribe amounted to two thousand. Be the deputies more or fewer, by the alterations which may happen in the progress of time, it disordereth nothing. Now to ascend by these stairs into the upper rooms of this building, it is proposed:

> 10. That the deputies elected in the several parishes, together with their magistrates and other officers, both civil and military, elected in their several hundreds, assemble

or muster annually; for example, upon
Monday next ensuing the last of February
at the capital of their tribe.

How the troops and companies of the deputies, with
their military officers or commanders thus assembled,
may without expense of time be forthwith distributed
into one uniform and orderly body, hath been elsewhere
shown and is not needful to be repeated. For their work,
which at this meeting will require two days, it is proposed:

11. That the whole body thus assembled, upon
the first of the assembly, elect out of the
horse of their number one high sheriff, one
lieutenant of the tribe, one custos rotulorum,
one conductor and two censors. That the high
sheriff be commander-in-chief, the lieutenant
commander in the second place, and the conductor in the third, of this band or squadron.
That the custos rotulorum be muster-master
and keep the rolls. That the censors be
governors of the ballot. And that the term
of these magistracies be annual.

These being thus elected, it is proposed:

12. That the magistrates of the tribe, that
is to say the high sheriff, lieutenant, custos
rotulorum, the censors and the conductors,
together with the magistrates and officers
of the hundreds, that is to say the twenty
justices of the peace, the forty jurymen,
the twenty high constables, be one troop,
or one troop and one company apart, called
the prerogative troop or company. That
this troops bring in and assist the justices
of assize, hold the quarter sessions in their
several capacities, and perform their other
functions as formerly.

By this means the commonwealth, at the introduction, may embrace the law as it stands, that is unreformed, which is to the greatest advantage of like
reformations; for to reform laws before the introduction of the government which is to show unto what
the laws in reformation are to be brought or fitted, is
impossible. But these magistrates of the hundreds and
tribes being such whereby the parliament is to govern

the nation, this is a regard in which they ought to be further capable of such orders and instructions as shall thereunto be requisite; for which cause it is proposed:

>13. That the magistrates of the tribe, that is to say the high sheriff, lieutenant, custos rotulorum, the censors and the conductors, together with the twenty justices elected at the hundreds, be a court for the government of the tribe called the phylarch; and that this court proceed, in all matter of government, and shall from time to time be directed by act of parliament.

By these courts the commonwealth will be furnished with true channels, whereby at leisure to turn the law into that which is sufficiently known to have been her primitive course, and into perfect reformation by degrees and without violence. For as the corruption of our law deriveth from an art enabled to improve her private interest, or from the law upon the bench and the jury at the bar; so the reformation of our law must come from disabling her as an art to improve her private interest, or to a jury upon the bench and the law at the bar, as in Venice.

<u>Judges and officers shall thou make thee in all thy gates which the Lord thy God giveth thee throughout thy tribes, and they shall judge the people with just judgment</u>. These courts, whose session house was in the gates of every city, were shown each of them to have consisted of twenty-three elders, which were as a jury upon the bench, giving sentence by plurality of votes, and under a kind of appeal unto the seventy elders or senate of Israel, as was also shown in the second book.

This or the like, by all example and beyond any controversy, hath been and is the natural way of judicature in commonwealths. The phylarchs, with a court or two of appeal, eligible out of the senate and the people, are at any time, with ease and with small alteration, to be cast upon a triennial rotation; which for the rest, proceeding after the manner of the Venetian <u>quarantie</u>, will be in this case perfect orders.*

SENATE AND MAGISTRATES

To return: the first day's election at the tribe

*The Art of Lawgiving.

being as hath been shown, it is proposed:

> 14. That the squadron of the tribe, upon the second day of their assembly, elect two knights and three burgesses out of the horse of their number, and four other burgesses out of the foot of their number. That each knight upon election forthwith make oath of allegiance unto the commonwealth or, refusing such oath, the next competitor in election to the same magistracy, making the said oath, be the magistrate; the like for the burgesses. That the knights thus sworn have session in the senate for the term of three years; and that the burgesses thus sworn be of the prerogative tribe, or representative of the people, for the like term.

Now whereas this proposition is sufficient for the perpetuation of the senate and the assembly of the people, being once instituted, but not sufficient for the full and perfect institution of them, it necessitateth the addition in this place, not of a permanent order, but of an expedient for the first year's election only; which may be this:

> That for the full and perfect institution of the assemblies mentioned, the squadron of the tribe, in the first year of the commonwealth, elect two knights for the term of one year, two other knights for the term of two years and lastly, two knights more for the term of three years; the like for the burgesses of the horse first, and then for those of the foot.

By this expedient, the senate in fifty tribes is constituted of three hundred knights or senators, whereof one hundred, through expiration of their terms, come annually to fall and another hundred at the same time to enter. The like for the prerogative tribe, or assembly of the people, which consisting in the whole of one thousand and fifty, suffers the like alteration in one third part, or in the yearly exchange of one hundred and fifty burgesses;* by which means the motion or rotation of these assemblies is annual, triennial and perpetual.

. . . .
*Harrington's math was incorrect. Total is 350 burgesses.

The senate and the congregation of representative of the people are in every commonwealth the main orders; the stairs or degrees of ascent unto these being now mounted, it remains that I lead unto the rooms of state, or the assemblies themselves; which shall be performed, first, by showing their frame and next, by showing their uses or functions. To bring you first into the senate, it is proposed:

16. That the knights of the annual election in the tribes take their places on Monday next ensuing the last of March in the senate. That the like number of knights, whose session determineth at the same time, recede. That every knight or senator be paid out of the public revenue quarterly one hundred twenty-five pounds during his term of session, and be obliged to sit in purple robes.

17. That annually, upon reception of the new knights, the senate proceed unto election of new magistrates and counsellors. That for magistrates they elect one general, one speaker and two censors, each for the term of one year, these promiscuously; and that they elect one commissioner of the great seal and one commissioner of the treasury, each for the term of three years and out of the new knights only.

This proposition supposeth the commissioners of the seal and those of the treasury to consist each of three, wheeled by the annual election of one into each order, upon a triennial rotation. For further explanation of the senatorian magistracies, it is proposed:

18. That the general and speaker, as counsuls of the commonwealth and presidents of the senate, be, during the term of their magistracy, paid quarterly five hundred pounds; that the ensigns of these magistracies be a sword borne before the general, and a mace before the speaker; that they be obliged to wear ducal robes; and that what is said of the general in this proposition, be understood only of the general sitting and not of the general marching.

19. That the general sitting, in case he be

commanded to march, receive field pay; and
that a new general be forthwith elected by
the senate to succeed him in the house, with
all the rights, ensigns and emoluments of the
general sitting; and this so often as one
or more generals are marching.

20. That the three commissioners of the great
seal, and the three commissioners of the
treasury, using their ensigns and habit and
performing their other functions as formerly,
be paid quarterly unto each of them three
hundred seventy-five pounds.

21. That the censors be each of them chancellor
of one university by virtue of their election;
that they govern the ballot, that they be
presidents of the council for religion, that
each have a silver wand for the ensign of his
magistracy, that each be paid quarterly three
hundred seventy-five prounds, and be obliged
to wear scarlet robes.

22. That the general sitting, the speaker
and the six commissioners abovesaid be the
signory of this commonwealth.*

Every monday morning, in the summer at seven and
in the winter at eight, the great bell in the clock-
house at the Pantheon /Westminster Hall/ beginneth,
and continueth ringing for the space of one hour, in
which time the magistrates of the senate, being attended according to their quality with a respective
number of the ballotines, door-keepers and messengers,
and having the ensigns of their magistracies borne
before them -- as the sword before the strategus, the
mace before the orator, a mace with the seal before the
commissioners of the chancery, the like with the purse
before the commissioners of the treasury, and a silver
wand, like those in use with the universities, before
each of the censors (being chancellors of the same) -
these, with the knights, in all three hundred, assemble
in the house or hall of the senate.

The house or hall of the senate /Westminster
Hall/, being situated in the Pantheon or palace of
justice, is a room consisting of a square and a half.

*The Art of Lawgiving.

In the middle of the lower end is the door; at the upper end hangeth a rich (canopied) state, over-shadowing the greater part of a large throne, or half pace of two stages, the first ascended by two steps from the floor and the second, about the middle, rising two steps higher. Upon this stand two chairs; in that on the right hand sits the strategus, in the other the orator, adorned with scarlet robes, after the fashion that was used by the dukes in the aristocracy. At the right end of the upper stage stand three chairs, in which the three commissioners of the seal are placed, and at the other end sit the three commissioners of the treasury, every one in a robe or habit like that of the earls; of these magistrates of this upper state consisteth the signory. At either end of the lower stage stands a little table, to which the secretaries of the senate are set, with their tufted sleeves in the habit of civil lawyers. Unto the four steps, whereby the two stages of the throne are ascended, answer four long benches which, successively deriving from every one of the steps, contain their respective height, and extend themselves by the side walls towards the lower end of the house, every bench being divided by numeral characters into the thirty-seven parts or places. Upon the upper benches sit the censors in the robes of barons; the first in the middle of the right-hand bench, and the second directly opposite unto him on the other side. Upon the rest of the benches sit the knights who, if they be called unto the urns, distributing themselves by the figures, come in equal files, either by the first seat, which consisteth of the two upper benches on either side, or by the second seat, consisting of the two lower benches on either side, beginning also at the upper or at the lower ends of the same, according to the lot whereby they are called, for which end the benches are open and ascended at either end with easy stairs and large passages. The rest of the ballot is conformable unto that of the tribe, the censors of the house sitting at the side urns, and the youngest magistrate of the signory at the middle; the urns being placed before the throne, and prepared according unto the number of the magistrates to be at that time chosen by the rules already given unto the censors of the tribes. But before the benches of the knights on either side stands one being shorter; and at the upper end of this, sit the two tribunes of the horse, at the upper end of the other the two tribunes of the foot, in their arms; the rest of the benches covered by the judges of the land in their robes; but these magistrates having no suffrage, neither the tribunes, though they derive their presence in the senate from the Romans, nor the judges, though they derive theirs from the ancient senate of Oceana. Every Monday, this assembly sits of course; at other times, if there be occasion, any magistrate of the house, by giving order for the bell, or by his lictor or ensign-bearer, calls a senate; and every magistrate or knight during his session hath the title, place and honour of a duke, earl, baron or knight respectively. And every one that hath borne the same magistracy tertio, by his third session, hath his respective place and title during the term of his life, which is all the honour conferred by this commonwealth, except upon the master of the ceremonies, the master of the horse and the king of the heralds, who are knights by their places. And thus you have the face of the senate, in which there is scarce any feature that is not Roman or Venetian; nor did the horns of this crescent extend themselves much unlike those of the Sanhedrim, on either hand of the prince and of the father of that senate. But upon beauty, in which every man hath his fancy, we will not otherwise philosophise than to remember that there is something more than decency in the robe of a judge that would not be well spared from the bench; and that the gravest magistrate unto whom you can commit the sword of justice will find a quickness in the spurs of honour which, if they be not laid unto virtue, will lay themselves unto that which may rout a commonwealth.

To come from the face of the senate unto the constitution and use of the parts, it is contained in the peculiar orders. And the orders which are peculiar unto the senate are either of election or instruction.

Elections in the senate are of three sorts, annual, biennial and extraordinary.

Annual elections are performed by the schedule called the tropic, and the tropic consisteth of two parts; the one containing the magistrates, and the other the councils, to be yearly elected. The schedule or tropic of the magistrates is as followeth in

The fifteenth order: requiring that upon every Monday next ensuing the last of March, the knights of the annual galaxies taking their places in the senate be called the first region of the same; and that the house, having dismissed the third region and received the first, proceed unto election of the magistrates contained in the first part of the tropic, by the ensuing schedule:

The lord strategus.	
The lord orator.	annual.
The first censor.	magistrates.
The second censor.	
The third commissioner of the seal.	triennial
The third commissioner of the treasury.	magistrates.

The annual magistrates (provided that no one man bear above one of those honours during the term of one session) may be elected out of any region. But the triennial magistrates may not be elected out of any other than the third region only, lest the term of their session expire before that of their honour and (it being unlawful for any man to bear magistracy any longer than he is thereunto qualified by the election of the people) cause a fraction in the rotation of this commonwealth.

The strategus is first president of the senate, and general of the army if it be commanded to march; in which case there shall be a second strategus elected to be first president of the senate, and general of the second army: and if this also be commanded to march a third strategus shall be chosen, and so as long as the commonwealth sendeth forth armies. The lord orator is second and more peculiar president of the senate, unto whom it appertaineth to keep the house unto orders.

The censors, whereof the first by consequence of his election is chancellor of the University of Clio and the second of that of Calliope, are presidents of the council for religion and magistrates, unto whom it belongeth to keep the house unto the order of the ballot. They are also inquisitors into the ways and means of acquiring magistracy, and have power to punish indirect proceeding in the same, by removing a knight or magistrate out of the house, under appeal unto the senate.

The commissioners of the seal, being three, whereof the third is annually chosen out of the third region, are judges in chancery.

The commissioners of the treasury, being three, whereof the third is annually chosen out of the third region, are judges in the exchequer; and every magistrate of this schedule hath right to propose unto the senate.

But the strategus with the six commissioners are the signory of this commonwealth, having right of session and suffrage in every council of the senate and power, either jointly, or severally, to propose in all or any of them.

. . . .

The twentieth order: containing the method of debate to be observed by the magistrates and the councils successively, in order to a decree of the senate.

The magistrates of the signory, as counsellors of this commonwealth, shall take into their consideration all matters of state or of government; and, having right to propose in any council, may any one or more of them propose what business he or they please in that council whereunto it most properly belongeth. And that the councils may be held unto their duty, the said magistrates are superintendents and inspectors of the same, with right to propose unto the senate.

The censors have equal power with these magistrates, but in relation unto the council of religion only.

Any two of three provosts in every council may propose to, and are the most peculiar proposers of, the same council; to the end that there be not only an inspection and superintendency of business in general, but that every work be also committed unto a peculiar hand.

Any one or more of the magistrates, or any two of the provosts respectively having proposed, the council shall debate the business so proposed, to which they of the third region that are willing shall speak first in their order; they of the second, next; and they of the first last; and the opinions of those that proposed or spoke, as they shall be thought the most considerable by the council, shall be taken by the secretary of the same in writing, and each of them signed with the name of the author.

The opinions being thus prepared, any magistrate of the signory, censor, or any two of the provosts of that council, upon this occasion may assemble the senate.

The senate being assembled, the opinions (for example, if they be four) shall be read in their order, that is according unto the order or dignity of the magistrates or counsellors by which they were signed. And being read, if any of the council introducing them will speak, they, as best acquainted with the business, shall have precedence, and after them the senators shall speak according unto their regions, beginning by the third first, and so continuing till every man that will have spoken: and when the opinions have been sufficiently debated, they shall be put all together unto the ballot after this manner.

Four secretaries, carrying each of them one of the opinions in one hand, with a white box in the other, and each following another (according unto the order of the opinions), shall present his box, naming the author of his opinion unto every senator; and one secretary or ballotine with a green box shall follow the four white ones; and one secretary or ballotine with a red box shall follow the green one; and every senator shall put one ball into some one of these six boxes. The suffrage being gathered and opened before the signory, if the red box or non-sincere had above half the suffrages, the opinions shall be all cast out, for the major part of the house is not clear in the business. If no one of the four opinions had above half the suffrages in the affirmative, that which had fewest shall be cast out, and the other three shall be ballotted again. If no one of the three had above half, that which had fewest shall be cast out, and the other two shall be ballotted again. If neither of the two had above half, that which had fewest shall be cast out, and the remaining opinion shall be ballotted again. And if the remaining opinion have not above half, it shall also be cast out. But the first of the opinions that arrives at most above half in the affirmative is the decree of the senate. The opinions being all of them cast out by the non-sincere may be reviewed (if occasion permit) by the council, and brought in again. If they be cast out by the negative, the case being of advice only, the house approveth not, and there is an end of it; the case being necessary, and admitting delay, the council is to think again upon the business and to bring in new opinions, but the case being necessary, and not admitting delay, the senate forthwith, electing the junta, shall create the dictator. <u>Et videat dictator ne quid respublica detrimenti capiat</u>.

This in case the debate conclude not in a decree; but if a decree be passed, it is either in matter of state, or government according to law enacted already, and then it is good without going any farther; or it is in matter of law to be enacted, repealed or amended, and then the degree of the senate, especially if it be for a war, or for a levy of men or money, is invalid without the result of the commonwealth, which is in the prerogative tribe, or representative of the people.

The senate, having prepared a decree to be proposed unto the people, shall appoint their proposers; and no other may propose for the senate unto the people but the magistrates of the house: that is to say the three commissioners of the seal, or any two of them, the three of the treasury, or any two of them, or the two censors.

The senate, having appointed their proposers, shall require of the tribunes a muster of the people at a set time and place; and, the tribunes, or any two of them, having mustered the people accordingly, the proposers shall propose the sense or decree of the senate by clauses unto the people. And that which is proposed by the authority of the senate, and resolved by the command of the people, is the law of Oceana.*

COUNCILS AND DICTATOR

For senatorian councils, it is proposed:

23. That there be a council of state consisting of fifteen knights, five out of each order or election; and that the same be perpetuated by the annual election of five out of the new knights or last elected into the senate.

24. That there be a council for religion, consisting of twelve knights, four out of each order, and perpetuated by the annual election of four out of the knights last elected into the senate. That there be a council for trade, consisting of a like number, elected and perpetuated in the same manner.

25. That there be a council of war, not elected by the senate, but elected by the council of state out of themselves. That this council of war consist of nine knights, three out of each order, and be perpetuated by the annual election of three out of the last knights elected into the council of state.

*The Commonwealth of Oceana.

26. That in case the senate add nine knights more out of their own number unto the council of war, the said council be understood by such addition to be dictator of the commonwealth, for the term of three months and no longer, except by farther order of the senate the said dictatorian power be prolonged for a like term.

27. That the signory have session and suffrage, with right also jointly or severally to propose both in the senate and in all senatorian councils.

28. That each of the three orders or divisions of knights in each senatorian council elect one provost for the term of one week; and that any two provosts of the same council so elected may propose unto their respective council, and not otherwise.

29. That some fair room or rooms, well furnished and attended, be allowed at the state's charge for a free and open academy unto all comers at some convenient hour or hours towards the evening. That this academy be governed according unto the rules of good breeding or civil conversation, by some or all of the proposers; and that in the same it be lawful for any man, by word of mouth or by writing, in jest or in earnest, to propose unto the proposers.*

The subject matter of the councils is distributed unto them by

The nineteenth order: distributing unto every council such businesses as are properly to belong unto their cognizance, whereof some they shall receive and determine, and others they shall receive, prepare and introduce into the house, as first:

The council of state to receive all addresses, intelligences and letters of negotiation; to give audience to ambassadors sent unto, and to draw up instructions for such as shall be sent by, this commonwealth; to receive

*The Art of Lawgiving.

propositions from, and hold intelligence with, the provincial councils; to consider upon all laws to be enacted, amended or repealed, and upon all levies of men or money, war or peace, leagues or associations to be made by this commonwealth, so far forth as is conducible unto the orderly preparation of the same, to be introduced by them into the senate. Provided that all such affairs as (otherwise appertaining unto the council of state) are, for the good of the commonwealth, to be carried with greater secrecy, be managed by the council of war, with power to receive and send forth agents, spies, emissaries, intelligencers, frigates, and to manage affairs of that nature, if it be necessary, without communication unto the senate, till such time as it may be had without detriment unto the business. But they shall have no power to engage the commonwealth in a war, without the consent of the senate and the people. It appertaineth also unto this council to take charge of the fleet as admiral, and of all storehouses, armories, arsenals and magazines appertaining unto this commonwealth. They shall keep a diligent record of the military expeditions from time to time reported by him that was strategus or general, or one of the pole-marchs, in that action, or at least so far forth as the experience of such commanders may tend unto the improvement of the military discipline, which they shall digest and introduce into the senate; and if the senate shall thereupon frame any article, they shall see that it be observed in the musters or education of the youth. And whereas the council of war is the sentinel or scout of this commonwealth, if any person or persons shall go about to introduce debate into any popular assembly of the same, or otherwise to alter the present government, or strike at the root of it, they shall apprehend, or cause to be apprehended, seized, imprisoned, and examine, arraign, acquit or condemn and cause to be executed any such person or persons, of their proper power and authority and without appeal.

The council of religion as the arbiter of this commonwealth in cases of conscience more peculiarly appertaining unto religion, Christian charity, and a pious life, shall have the care of the national religion and the protection of the liberty of conscience, with the cognizance of all cases relating unto either of them. And first as to the national religion: they shall cause all places or preferments of the best revenue in either of the universities to be conferred upon none other than such of the most learned and pious men as have dedicated themselves unto the study of theology. They shall also take an especial care that by such augmentations as be or shall hereafter be appointed by the senate, every benefice in this nation be improved at the least unto the value of one hundred pounds a year. And to the end that there be no interest at all whereby the divines or teachers of the national religion may be corrupted or corrupt religion, they shall be capable of no other kind of employment or preferment in this commonwealth. And whereas a directory for the administration of the national religion is to be prepared by this council, they shall in this and other debates of this nature proceed in manner following: a question arising in matter of religion shall be put and stated by the council in writing, which writing the censors shall send by their beadles (being proctors chosen to attend them), each unto the university whereof he is chancellor; and the vice-chancellor of the same, receiving the writing, shall call a convocation of all the divines of that university being above forty years of age. And the universities upon a point so proposed shall have no manner of intelligence or correspondence one with another until their debates be ended, and they have made return of their answers unto the council of religion by two or three of their own members that may clear their sense, if any doubt should arise, unto the council; which done, they shall return and the council, having received such information, shall proceed according unto their own judgments in the preparation of the whole matter for the senate; that so, the interest of the learned being removed, there may be a right application of reason unto Scripture, which is the foundation of the national religion.

Secondly, this council, as to the protection of the liberty of conscience, shall suffer no coercive power in the matter of religion to be exercised in this nation; the teachers of the national religion being no other than such as voluntarily undertake that calling, and their auditors or hearers no other than are also voluntary. Nor shall any gathered congregation be molested or interrupted in their way of worship (being neither Jewish nor idolatrous) but vigilantly and vigorously protected and defended in the enjoyment, practice and profession of the same. And if there be officers or auditors appointed by such congregation, for the introduction of causes into the council of religion, all such causes so introduced shall be received, heard and determined by the same (with recourse had if need be unto the senate).

Thirdly, every petition addressed unto the senate, except that of a tribe, shall be received, examined and debated by this council; and such only as they upon such examination and debate had shall think fit may be introduced into the senate.

The council of trade, being the vena porta of this nation, shall hereafter receive instructions more at large. For the present, their experience attaining unto a right understanding of those trades and mysteries that feed the veins of this commonwealth, and a true distinction of them from those that suck or exhaust the same, they shall acquaint the senate with the conveniences and inconveniences, to the end that encouragement may be applied unto the one and remedy to the other.

The academy of the provosts being the affability of the commonwealth, shall assemble every day towards the evening in a fair room, having certain withdrawing rooms thereunto belonging. And all sorts of company that will repair thither for conversation or discourse, so it be upon the matter of government, news or intelligence, or to propose any thing unto the councils, shall be freely and affably received in the outer chamber and heard in the way of civil conversation, which is to be managed without any other awe or ceremony than thereunto is usually appertaining; to the end that every man may be free, and that what is proposed by one may be argued or discoursed upon by the rest, except the matter be of secrecy; in which case the provosts, or some of them, shall take such as desire audience into one of the withdrawing rooms. And the provosts are to give their minds that this academy be so governed, adorned and preserved, as may be most attractive unto men of parts and good affections unto the commonwealth, for the excellency of the conversation.

Furthermore, if any man, not being able or willing to come in person, have any advice to give which he judgeth may be for the good of the commonwealth, he may write his mind unto the academy of the provosts, in a letter signed or not signed, which letter shall be left with the door-keeper of the academy. Nor shall any person delivering such a letter be seized, molested or detained, though it should prove to be a libel. But the letters so delivered shall be presented unto the provosts; and in case they be so many that they cannot well be examined by the provosts themselves, they shall distribute them as they please to be read by the gentlemen of the academy who, finding anything in them material, will find matters of discourse; or, if they happen upon a business that requires privacy, return it with a note upon it unto a provost. And the provosts by the secretaries attending shall cause such notes out of discourses or letters to be taken as they please, to the end that they may propose, as occasion serveth, what any two of them shall think fit, out of their notes so taken, unto their respective councils; to the end that not only the ear of the commonwealth be open unto all, but that, men of such education being in her eye, she may upon emergent elections or occasions be always provided of her choice of fit persons.

Every council, being adorned with a state for the signory, shall be attended by two secretaries, two door-keepers and two messengers in ordinary, and have power to commend more upon emergencies, as occasion requireth. And the academy shall be attended with two secretaries, two messengers and two door-keepers; this with the other councils being provided with their farther conveniences at the charge of the state.

But whereas it is incident unto commonwealths upon emergencies requiring extraordinary speed or secrecy, either through their natural delays or unnatural haste to incur equal danger, while holding unto the slow pace of their orders they come not in time to defend themselves from some sudden blow, or breaking them for the greater speed they but haste unto their own destruction; if the senate shall at any time make election of nine knights extraordinary to be added unto the council of war, as a <u>junta</u> for the term of three months, the council of war, with the <u>junta</u> so added, is for the term of the same <u>dictator</u> of Oceana, having power to levy men and money, to make war and peace, as also to enact laws which shall be good for the space of one year (if they be not sooner repealed by the senate and the people) and for no longer time, except they be confirmed by the senate and the people. And the whole administration of the commonwealth for the term of the said three months shall be in the dictator; provided that the dictator shall have no power to do anything that tendeth not unto his proper end and institution, but all unto the preservation of the commonwealth as it is established and for the sudden restitution of the same unto the natural channel and common course of government. And all acts, orders, decrees or laws of the council of war with the <u>junta</u>, being thus created, shall be signed: <u>Dictator</u> <u>Oceanae</u>.*

*The Commonwealth of Oceana.

This dictatorian council (as may already appear) consisteth fundamentally of the signory with nine knights elected by the council of state, additionally of nine knights more emergently chosen by the senate and of the four tribunes of course, as will appear when I come to speak of that magistracy. Now if dictatorian power be indeed formidable, yet this in the first place is remarkable, that the council here offered for a dictator is of far safer constitution than what among us hitherto hath been offered for a commonwealth; has namely, a parliament, and a council in the interim. For here is no interim, but all the councils of the commonwealth not only remaining, but remaining in the exercise of all their functions, without the abatement of any; speed and secrecy belonging not unto any of their functions, but to that only of the dictator. And if this dictatorian council have more in it of a commonwealth than hath hitherto among us been either practised or offered, by what argument can it be pretended that a commonwealth is so imperfect through the necessity of such an order, that she must needs borrow of monarchy, seeing every monarchy that hath any senate, assembly or council in it, thereby most apparently borroweth more of a commonwealth than there is to be found of monarchy in this council?

. . . .

The dictator, being created, hath sovereign power in carrying on the orders of the commonwealth, but those do not perpetuate their power; this therefore cannot be done by force of arms. The arms of the commonwealth are both numerous, and in posture or readiness, but they consist of her citizens; and for the dictator to bring the citizens to break the commonwealth were for a general to command his army to cut their own throats. It is true the Roman decemvirs put in for prolongation; but, though in the most unequal commonwealth, could not make it stand one year, because of the citizens in arms. And for mercenaries, there are none in Oceana; is this news? There were none in Israel, there were none in Athens, there were none in Lacedaemon, there were none in Rome, while those commonwealths flourished. But were there mercenaries, as he might perhaps reckon servants, they are unarmed, undisciplined; they cannot rise, through the vast bodies of citizens in arms, both elders and youth; or, if they would rise, were nothing in their hands. The Roman slaves and the Lacedaemonian helots, being far of another and more dangerous nature, never rose against their lords but to their own destruction. All this while I say nothing of the security which is in the frame of this dictator, beyond any example or interest or prolongation to be found either in the Roman dictator or the Venetian Council of Ten, each whereof, having had like power, did never discover any such inclination. It is true that in the time of Sulla the Roman dictator began to be perpetual; but this is not to be attributed so much unto the imperfection of the order as to the change of the balance. But if the dictator of Oceana cannot have the interest, or having the interest cannot have the power or strength, to perpetuate that magistracy, much less can the senate.*

PREROGATIVE ASSEMBLY

Debate is the natural parent of result; whence the senate throughout Latin authors is called fathers, and throughout Greek authors the compellation of a popular assembly is men, as 'men of Athens', 'men of Corinth', 'men of Lacedaeman'; nor is this custom heathen only, seeing these compellations are used unto the senate and the people of the Jews, not only by Stephen but also by Paul, where they begin their speeches in this manner: men, brethren, and fathers. To come then from the fathers unto the people, popular assembly or prerogative tribe, it is proposed:

35. That the burgesses of the annual election returned by the tribes enter into the prerogative tribe upon Monday next ensuing the last of March; and that the like number of burgesses whose term is expired recede at the same time. That the burgesses thus entered elect unto themselves out of their own number two of the horse, one to be captain and the other to be cornet of the same; and two of the foot, one to be captain, the other to be ensign of the same, each for the term of three years. That these officers being thus elected, the whole tribe or assembly proceed to the election of four annual magistrates: two out of the foot, to be tribunes of the foot, and two out of the horse, to be tribunes of the horse. That the tribunes be commanders of this tribe in chief, so far as it is a military

*The Art of Lawgiving.

body, and presidents of the same as it is a civil assembly. And lastly, that this whole tribe be paid weekly as followeth: unto each of the tribunes of the horse, seven pound; unto each of the tribunes of foot, six pound; unto each of the captains of horse, five pound; unto each of the captains of foot, four pound; unto each of the cornets, three pound; unto each of the ensigns, two pound seven shillings; unto every horseman two pound; and to every one of the foot one pound ten shillings.

. . . .

38. That the right of debate, as also of proposing to the people, be wholly and only in the senate, without any power at all of result not derived from the people.

39. That the power of result be wholly and only in the people, without any right at all of debate.

40. That the senate, having debated and agreed upon a law to be proposed, cause promulgation of the same to be made for the space of six weeks before proposition; that is, cause the law to be printed and published so long before it is to be proposed.

41. That, promulgation being made, the signory demand of the tribunes being present in the senate an assembly of the people. That the tribunes, upon such demand of the signory or of the senate, be obliged to assemble the prerogative tribe in arms by sound of trumpet, with drums beating and colours flying, in any town, field or market-place being not above six miles distance, upon the day and at the hour appointed, except the meeting through inconvenience of the weather or the like be prorogued by consent of the signory and the tribunes. That, the prerogative tribe being assembled accordingly, the senate propose to them by two or more of the senatorian magistrates, thereunto appointed at the first promulgation of the law. That the proposers for the senate open unto the people the occasion, motives and reasons of the law to be proposed; and, the

same being done, put it by distinct clauses unto the ballot of the people. That if any material clause or clauses be rejected by the people, they be reviewed by the senate, altered and proposed, if they think fit, to the third time but no oftener.

42. That what is thus proposed by the senate, and resolved by the people, be the law of the land, and no other, except as in the case reserved unto the dictatorian council.

The twenty-third order: showing the power, function, and manner of proceeding of the prerogative tribe.

The power or function of the prerogative is of two parts: the one of result, in which it is the legislative power, the other of judicature, in which regard it is the highest court and the last appeal in this commonwealth.

For the former part, the people by this constitution being not obliged by any law that is not of their own making or confirmation by the result of the prerogative, their equal representative, it shall not be lawful for the senate to require obedience from the people, not for the people to give due obedience unto the senate, in or by any law that hath not been promulgated or printed and published for the space of six weeks and afterwards proposed by the authority of the senate unto the prerogative tribe, and resolved by the major vote of the same in the affirmative. Nor shall the senate have any power to levy war, men or money, otherwise than by the consent of the people so given, or by a law so enacted, except in cases of exigence, in which it is agreed that the power, both of the senate and the people, shall be in the dictator, so qualified and for such a term of time as is according unto that constitution already prescribed. While a law is in promulgation the censors shall animadvert upon the senate, and the tribunes upon the people, that there be no laying of heads together, conventicles or canvassing to carry

*The Art of Lawgiving.

on or oppose anything, but that all may be
done in a free and open way.

For the latter part of the power of the
prerogative, or that whereby they are the
supreme judicatory of this nation, and of
the provinces of the same, the cognizance of
crimes against the majesty of the people, as
high treason, as also of peculation, that
is robbery of the treasury or defraudation
of the commonwealth, appertaineth unto this
tribe, and if any person or persons, provincials or citizens, shall appeal unto the
people, it belongeth unto the prerogative
to judge and determine the case; provided
that if the appeal be from any court of
justice in this nation or the provinces, the
appellant shall first deposit one hundred
pounds in the court from which he appealeth,
to be forfeited unto the same if he be cast
in his suit by the people. But the power of
the council of war, being the expedition of
this commonwealth, and the martial law of the
strategus in the field, are those only from
which there shall lie no appeal unto the people.

The proceeding of the prerogative, in case of
a proposition, is to be thus ordered: the
magistrates, proposing by authority of the
senate, shall rehearse the whole matter and
expound it unto the people: which done, they
shall put the whole together unto the suffrage with three boxes, the negative, the affirmative, and the non-sincere, and the suffrage being returned unto the tribunes, and
numbered in the presence of the proposers, if
the major vote be in the non-sincere, the
proposers shall desist and the senate shall
resume the debate. If the major vote be in the
negative, the proposers shall desist, and the
senate too. But if the major vote be in the
affirmative, then the tribe is clear, and the
proposers shall begin and put the whole matter,
with the negative and the affirmative (leaving
out the non-sincere) by clauses; and the suffrages, being taken and numbered by the tribunes unto the senate; and that which is proposed by the authority of the senate, and confirmed by the command of the people, is the

law of Oceana.

The proceeding of the prerogative in a case of judicature is to be thus ordered. The tribunes, being auditors of all causes appertaining unto the cognizance of the people, shall have notice of the suit or trial, whether of appeal or otherwise, that is to be commenced, and if any one of them shall accept of the same it appertaineth unto him to introduce it. A cause being introduced and the people mustered or assembled for the decision of the same, the tribunes are presidents of the court, having power to keep it unto orders, and shall be seated upon a scaffold erected in the middle of the tribe; upon the right hand shall stand a seat or large pulpit, assigned unto the plaintiff or the accuser, and upon the left another for the defendant, each if they please with his counsel. And the tribunes, being attended upon such occasions with so many ballotines, secretaries, door-keepers and messengers of the senate as shall be requisite, one of them shall turn up a glass of the nature of an hour-glass, but such an one as is to be of an hour and a half's running; which being turned up, the party or counsel on the right hand may begin to speak to the people. If there be papers to be read, or witnesses to be examined, the officer shall lay the glass sideways until the papers be read and the witnesses examined, and then turn it up again; and so long as the glass is running the party on the right hand hath liberty to speak, and no longer. The party on the right hand having had his time, the like shall be done in every respect for the party on the left. And the cause being thus heard, the tribunes shall put the question unto the tribe with a white, a black and a red box (or non-sincere): whether guilty, or not guilty. And if, the suffrage being taken, the major vote be in the non-sincere, the cause shall be reheard upon the next juridical day following and put unto the question in the same manner. If the major vote come the second time in the non-sincere, the cause shall be heard again upon the third day; but at the third hearing the question shall be put without the non-sincere. Upon the first of the three days in which the major vote comes in the white box, the party accused is absolved; and upon the first of them in which it comes in the black box, the party accused is condemned. The party accused being condemned, the tribunes, if the case be criminal, shall put with the white and the black box these questions, or such of them as, regard had unto the case, they shall conceive most proper.

1. Whether he shall have a writ of ease.

2. Whether he shall be fined so much, or so much.

3. Whether he shall be confiscated.

4. Whether he shall be rendered incapable of magistracy.

5. Whether he shall be banished.

6. Whether he shall be put to death.

These or any three of these questions, whether simple or such as shall be thought fitly mixed, being put by the tribunes, that which hath most above half the votes in the black box is the sentence of the people, which the troop of the third <u>classis</u> is to see executed accordingly.

But whereas by the constitution of this commonwealth it may appear that neither the propositions of the senate, nor the judicature of the people, will be so frequent as to hold the prerogative in continual employment; the senate, a main part of whose office it is to teach and instruct the people, shall duly (if they have no greater affairs to divert them) cause an oration to be made unto the prerogative by some knight or magistrate of the senate, to be chosen out of the ablest men, and from time to time appointed by the orator of the house, in the great hall of the Pantheon /Westminster/ while the parliament resideth in the town; or

in some grove or sweet place in the field,
while the parliament for the heat of the year
shall reside in the country; upon every Tuesday
morning or afternoon.

And the orator appointed <u>pro tempore</u> unto
this office shall first repeat the orders of
the commonwealth with all possible brevity,
and then, making choice of one, or some part
of it, discourse thereof unto the people. An
oration or discourse of this nature, being
afterward perused by the council of state,
may as they see cause be printed and published.

The Archon's comment upon this order I find to
have been of this sense:

My lords:

To crave pardon for a word or two in further
explanation of what was read, I shall briefly
show how the constitution of this tribe or
assembly answers unto their function, and
how their function, which is of two parts,
the former in the result or legislative
power, the latter in the supreme judicature
of the commonwealth, answers unto their constitution. Machiavel /Machivaelli/ hath a
discourse, where he puts the question, whether
the guard of liberty be with more security to
be committed unto the nobility, or to be
people. Which doubt of his ariseth through
the want of explaining his term, for 'the
guard of liberty' can signify nothing else
but the result of the commonwealth; so that
to say that the guard of liberty may be
committed unto the nobility is to say that
the result may be committed unto the senate,
in which case the people signify nothing.
Now to show it was a mistake to affirm it
to have been thus in Lacedaemon /Sparta,
Greece/, sufficient hath been spoken; and
whereas he will have it to be so in Venice
also, 'quello', saith Contarini, '<u>appresso il
quale e la somma autorita di tutta la citta
e dalle leggi e decreti dei quali pende
l'autorita cosi del senato come ancora di
tutti i magistrati, e il consiglio grande</u>'.
It is institutively in the great council by

82

the judgment of all that know that commonwealth, though for the reasons shown it be sometimes exercised by the senate. Nor need I run over the commonwealths in this place for the proof of a thing so doubtless, and such as hath been already made so apparent, as that the result of each was in the popular part of it. The popular part of yours, or the prerogative tribe, consisteth of seven deputies (whereof three are of the horse) annually elected out of every tribe of Oceana, which being fifty, amounteth unto one hundred and fifty horse and two hundred foot; and the prerogative, consisting of three of these lists, consisteth of four hundred and fifty horse, and six hundred foot (besides those of the provinces to be hereafter mentioned), by which means, the over-balance in the suffrage remaining unto the foot by one hundred and fifty votes, you have, unto the support of a true and natural aristocracy, the deepest root of a democracy that hath been planted. Wherefore there is nothing in art of nature better qualified for the result than this assembly. It is noted out of Cicero by Machiavel /Machiavelli/ that the people, albeit they are not so prone to find out the truth of themselves, as to follow custom or run into error, yet, if they be shown truth, they are the most constant and faithful guardians and conservators of it. It is your duty and office, whereunto you are also qualified by the orders of this commonwealth, to have the people, as you have your hawks and greyhounds, in leases and slips, to range the fields and beat the bushes for them. For they are of a nature that is never good at this sport; but when you spring or start their proper quarry, think not that they will stand to ask you what it is, or less know it than the hawks and greyhounds do theirs, but forthwith make such a flight or course that a huntsman may as well undertake to run with his dogs, or a falconer to fly with his hawk, as an aristocracy at this game to compare with the people. The people of Rome were seized upon no less prey than the empire of the world, when the nobility turned tails and perched among daws upon the tower of monarchy. For though they did not all of them intend the thing, they would none of them endure the remedy, which was the agrarian.

But the prerogative tribe hath not only the result, but in the supreme judicature and the ultimate appeal in this commonwealth. For the popular government that makes account to be of any standing must make sure in the first place of the appeal unto the people. <u>Ante omnes de provocatione adversus magistratus ad populum, sacrandoque cum bonis capite ejus, qui regni occupandi concilia inesset</u>. As an estate in trust become a man's own if he be not answerable for it, so, the power of a magistracy not accountable unto the people from whom it was received becoming of private use, the commonwealth loses her liberty. Wherefore the right of supreme judicature in the people (without which there can be no such thing as popular government) is confirmed by the constant practice of all commonwealths, as that of Israel in the cases of Achan and of the tribe of Benjamin, adjudged by the congregation.*

RELIGION

9. Democracy, being nothing but entire liberty - and liberty of conscience without civil liberty, or civil liberty without liberty of conscience, being but liberty by halves - must admit of liberty of conscience, both as to the perfection of its present being, and as to its future security; as to the perfection of its present being, for the reasons already shown, or that she do not enjoy liberty by halves; and for future security, because this excludes absolute monarchy, which cannot stand with liberty of conscience in the whole, and regulated monarchy, which cannot stand safely with it in any part.

10. If it be said that in France there is liberty of conscience in part, it is also plain that while the hierarchy is standing this liberty is falling, and that if ever it comes to pull down the hierarchy, it pulls down that monarchy also; wherefore the monarchy or hierarchy will be beforehand with it, if they see their

*The Commonwealth of Oceana.

true interest.

11. The ultimate result in monarchy being that of one man, or of a few men, the national religion in monarchy may happen not to be the religion of the major part of the people; but the result in democracy being in the major part of the people, it cannot happen but that the national religion must be that of the major part of the people.

12. The major part of the people, being in matters of religion enabled to be their own leaders, will in such cases therefore have a public leading; or, being debarred of their will in that particular, are debarred of their liberty of conscience.

13. Where the major part of the people is debarred of their liberty by the minor, there is neither liberty of conscience nor democracy, but spiritual or civil oligarchy.

14. Where the major part is not debarred of their liberty of conscience by the minor, there is a national religion.*

There is nothing more certain or demonstrable unto common sense than that the far greater part of mankind, in matter of religion, give themselves up unto the public leading. Now a national religion, rightly established, or not coercive, is not any public driving, but only the public leading. If the public in this case may not lead such as desire to be led by the public, and yet a party may lead such as desire to be led by a party, where would be the liberty of conscience as to the state? Which certainly in a well-ordered commonwealth, being the public reason, must be the public conscience. Nay, where would be the liberty of conscience as to any party which should so proceed as to show that, without taking the liberty of conscience from others, they think not that they can have it themselves? If the public, refusing the liberty of conscience unto a party, would but be the cause of tumult, how much more a party refusing it unto the public? And how, in case of like tumult, should a party defend their liberty of conscience, or indeed their throats, from the whole or a far greater party, without keeping down or tyrannising over the whole or a far greater party

*A System of Politics.

by force of arms? These things being rightly considered, it is no wonder that men, living like men, have not been yet found without a government, or that government hath not been yet found without a national religion; that is, some orderly and known way of public leading in divine things, or in the worship of God.

A national religion being thus proved necessary, it remaineth that I prove what is necessary unto a national religion, that is, as to the state or in relation unto the duty of the magistrate.

Certain it is that religion hath not seen corruption but by one of three causes: some interest therewithal incorporated, some ignorance of the truth of it, or by some complication of both. Nor was ever religion left wholly unto a clergy that escaped these causes, or their most pernicious effects; as in Rome, which hath brought ignorance to be the mother of devotion, and indeed interest to be the father of religion. Now, the clergy not failing in this case to be dangerous, what recourse but to the magistrate for safety? Especially seeing these causes, that is, interest and ignorance - the one deriving from evil laws, the other from the want of good education - are not in the right or power of a clergy, but of a magistracy. Or if so it be that magistrates of bounded duty ought to be nursing fathers and nursing mothers unto the church, how shall a state in the sight of God be excusable that taketh no heed or care lest religion suffer by causes the prevention or remedy whereof is in them only? To these therefore it is proposed:

> 46. That the universities, being prudently reformed, be preserved in their rights and endowments, for and towards the education and provision of an able ministry.

We are commanded by Christ to <u>search the Scriptures</u>. The Scriptures are not now to be searched but by skill in tongues. The immediate gift of tongues is ceased; how then should skill in tongues be acquired but mediately, or by the means of education? How should a state expect such education (especially for a matter of ten thousand men) that provideth not for it? And what provision can a state make for such education but by such schools, so endowed and regulated, as with us are the universities? These therefore are a necessary step towards the prevention of such ignorance or interest as, through the infirmities or bias of translators, interpreters and preachers, both have and may frequently come to be incorporated with religion; as also unto the improvement or acquisition of such light as is by the command of Christ to be attained or exercised in searching the Scriptures.

The excellent learning of the Levites in all kinds, not ordinarily infused but acquired, there having been among them as well the teacher as the scholar, leaveth little doubt but their forty-eight cities were as so many universities. These, with their suburbs or endowments, contained in the whole (each of their circuits in land reckoned at four thousand cubits deep) about an hundred thousand acres; that is, if their measure were according to the common cubit; if according to the holy cubit (as with Levites was most likely) twice so much; which at the lowest account I conceive to be far above the revenues of both our universities.

These being ordered as hath been said, it is proposed:

47. That the legal and ancient provision for the national ministry be so augmented that the meanest sort of livings or benefices, without defalcation from the greater, be each improved to the revenue of one hundred pounds a year at the least.

This, in regard the way is by tithes, cometh up so close unto the orders of Israel as in our days show that a commonwealth may come too near that pattern to be liked. We find not indeed that the apostles either took or demanded tithes; in which case the priests, who were legally possessed of them, might have suspicion that they, under colour of religion, had aimed at the violation of property. But putting the case that generally the priests had been converted unto the Christian faith, whether would the apostles for that reason have enjoined them to relinquish their tithes? Or what is there in the Christian religion to favour any such surmise? To me there seemeth to be abundantly enough to the contrary. For if the apostles stuck not to comply with the Jews in a ceremony which was of mere human invention, and to introduce this, as they did ordination, by imposition of hands into the Christian church; that they would, upon like inducement, have refused a standing law, undoubtedly Mosaical, is in my opinion most improbable. So that, I conceive, the law for tithes in being may or may not be continued, at the pleasure of the lawgivers, for anything in this case to the contrary. Confident I am that the introducing of this model in the whole, which is thought so impracticable, were not unto willing minds so difficult a work as the abolition of tithes.

But benefices, whether by way of tithes or otherwise, being thus ordered, it is proposed:

48. That, a benefice becoming void in any parish, the elders of the same may assemble and give notice unto the vice-chancellor of either university by certificate, specifying the true value of that benefice; that the vice-chancellor, upon receipt of such certificate, be obliged to call a congregation of his university; that the congregation of the university to this end assembled, having regard unto the value of the benefice, make choice of a person fitted for the ministerial function, and return him unto the parish so requiring; that the probationer, thus returned unto a parish by either of the universities, exercise the office and receive the benefits as minister of the parish for the term of one year; that, the term of one year expired, the elders of the parish assemble and put the election of the probationer unto the ballot; that if the probationer have three parts in four of the balls or votes in the affirmative, he be thereby ordained and elected minister of that parish, not afterwards to be degraded or removed but by the censors of the tribe, the phylarch of the same, or the council of religion in such cases as shall be unto them reserved by act of parliament. That in case the probationer come to fail of three parts in four at the ballot, he depart from that parish; and if he return unto the university, it be without diminution of the former offices or preferments which he there enjoyed, or any prejudice unto his future preferment; and that it be lawful in this case for any parish to send so often unto either university, and be the duty of either vice-chancellor upon such certificates to make return of different probationers, till such time as the elders of that parish have fitted themselves with a

minister of their own choice and liking.

In case it were thought fit that a probationer thus elected should before he depart, receive imposition of hands by the doctors of the university; I cannot see what the most scrupulous in the matter of ordination could find wanting. But be this so, or otherwise. The universities, by proposing unto the congregation in every parish, do the senatorian office; and the people, thus fitting themselves by their suffrage or ballot, reserve that office which is truly popular, that is the result, unto themselves.

Moses (for so far divines reach at ordination) in the institution of the senate of Israel, wherein he can never be proved to have used imposition of hands, doing the senatorian office, caused the people to take wise men, and understanding, and known among the tribes, whereof the lot fell upon all but Aldad and Medad. And the apostles, doing the senatorian office in like manner, without imposition of hands, caused the whole congregation to take two, whereof the lot of apostleship fell upon Matthias. So that this way of ordination, being that which was instituted by Moses, and the prime of those which were taken up by the apostles, is both Mosaical and apostolical. Nor hath a well-ordered commonwealth any choice of those other ways of ordination, used by the apostles in compliance unto worse government, but is naturally necessitated unto this, that is unto the very best.

Ordination being thus provided for, it is proposed:

49. That the national religion be exercised according to a directory in that case, to be made and published by act of parliament. That the national ministry be permitted to have no other public preferment or office in this commonwealth. That a national minister, being convicted of ignorance or scandal, be movable out of his benefice by the censors of the tribe, under an appeal unto the phylarch or to the council for religion.

50. That no religion being contrary unto or destructive of Christianity, nor the public exercise of any religion being grounded upon or incorporated into a foreign interest, be

protected by or tolerated in this state.
That all other religions, with the public
exercise of the same, be both tolerated and
protected by the council of religion; and
that all professors of any such religion be
equally capable of all elections, magistracies,
preferments and offices in this commonwealth,
according unto the orders of the same.

Upon the whole of these propositions touching
church discipline: thus neither would the party that is
for gifted men through ignorance (which else in all probability they must) lose religion, nor the clergy corrupt
it through interest. But decency and order, with the
liberty of conscience, would still flourish together,
while the minister hath a preferment he sought, the
parish a minister they chose, the nation a religion according to the public conscience, and every man his
Christian liberty.

The council of religion as the arbiter
of this commonwealth in cases of conscience
more peculiarly appertaining unto religion,
Christian charity, and a pious life, shall
have the care of the national religion and
the protection of the liberty of conscience,
with the cognizance of all causes relating
unto either of them. And first as to the
national religion: they shall cause all places
or preferments of the best revenue in either
of the universities to be conferred upon none
other than such of the most learned and pious
men as have dedicated themselves unto the
study of theology. They shall also take an
especial care that by such augmentations as
be or shall hereafter be appointed by the
senate, every benefice in this nation be improved at the least unto the value of one
hundred pounds a year. And to the end that
there be no interest at all whereby the
divines or teachers of the national religion
may be corrupted or corrupt religion, they
shall be capable of no other kind of employment or preferment in this commonwealth.
And whereas a directory for the administration
of the national religion is to be prepared by
this council, they shall in this and other

*The Art of Lawgiving.

debates of this nature proceed in manner following: a question arising in matter of religion shall be put and stated by the council in writing, which writing the censors shall send by their beadles (being proctors chosen to attend them), each unto the university whereof he is chancellor; and the vice-chancellor of the same, receiving the writing, shall call a convocation of all the divines of that university being about forty years of age. And the universities upon a point so proposed shall have no manner of intelligence or correspondence one with another until their debates be ended, and they have made return of their answers unto the council of religion by two or three of their own members that may clear their sense, if any doubt should arise, unto the council; which done, they shall return and the council, having received such information, shall proceed according unto their own judgments in the preparation of the whole matter for the senate; that so, the interest of the learned being removed, there may be a right application of reason unto Scripture, which is the foundation of the national religion.

Secondly, this council, as to the protection of the liberty of conscience, shall suffer no coercive power in the matter of religion to be exercised in this nation; the teachers of the national religion being no other than such as voluntarily undertake the calling, and their auditors or hearers no other than are also voluntary. Nor shall any gathered congregation be molested or interrupted in their way of worship (being neither Jewish nor idolatrous) but vigilantly and vigorously protected and defended in the enjoyment, practice and profession of the same. And if there be officers or auditors appointed by any such congregation, for the introduction of causes into the council of religion, all such causes so introduced shall be received, heard and determined by the same (with recourse had if need be unto the senate).*

*The Commonwealth of Oceana.

MILITARY ESTABLISHMENT

The military part, on which at present I shall discourse little, consisteth in the discipline of the youth, that is of such as are between eighteen and thirty years of age; and for the discipline of the youth it is proposed:

> 51. That annually upon Wednesday next ensuing the last of December, the youth of each parish (under the inspection of the two overseers of the same) assemble and elect the fifth man of their number, or one in five of them, to be for the term of that year deputies of the youth of that parish.
>
> 52. That annually on Wednesday next ensuing the last of January, the said deputies of the respective parishes meet at the capital of the hundred (where there are games and prizes allotted for them, as hath been shown elsewhere); that there they elect to themselves out of their own number one captain and one ensign. And that of these games and this election, the magistrates and officers of the hundred be presidents and judges for the impartial distribution of the prizes.
>
> 53. That annually upon Wednesday next ensuing the last of February, the youth through the whole tribe, thus elected, be received at the capital of the same, by the lieutenant as commander-in-chief, by the conductor and by the censors; that under inspection of these magistrates, the said youth be entertained with more splendid games, disciplined in a more military manner, and divided by lot into sundry parts or essays, according to rules elsewhere given.
>
> 54. That the whole youth of the tribe, thus assembled, be the first essay. That out of the first essay there be cast by lot two hundred horse and six hundred foot; that they whom their friends will or themselves can mount be accounted horse, the rest foot. That these forces, amounting in the fifty tribes to ten thousand horse

and thirty thousand foot, be always ready
to march at a week's warning; and that this
be the second essay, or the standing army
of the commonwealth.

55. That for the holding of each province /̄Scotland and Ireland/̄, the commonwealth in the first year assign an army of the youth, consisting of seven thousand five hundred foot and one thousand five hundred horse. That for the perpetuation of these provincial armies or guards, there be annually, at the time and places mentioned, cast out of the first essay of the youth in each tribe, ten horse and fifty foot, that is in all the tribes five hundred horse and two thousand five hundred foot for Scotland, the like for Ireland; and the like of both orders for the sea-guards, being each obliged to serve for the term of three years upon the state's pay.

The standing army of the commonwealth consisting thus of forty thousand, not soldiers of fortune, not in body nor in pay, but citizens at their vocations or trades, and yet upon command in continual readiness; and the provincial armies each consisting of nine thousand in pay in body, and possessed of the avenues and places of strength in the province, it is not imaginable how a province should be so soon able to stir, as the commonwealth must be to pour forty thousand men upon it, besides the sea-guards. Nor cometh this militia thus constituted, except upon marches, unto any charge at all; the standing army having no pay, and the provinces, whereof the sea thus guarded will be none of the poorest, maintaining their own guards. Such is the military way of a commonwealth and the constitution of her armies, whether levied by suffrage as in Rome, or lot as in Israel......

Standing forces being thus established for such as are upon emergent occasions to go forth or march, it is proposed:

56. That the senate and the people, or the dictator, having decreed or declared war, and the field officers being appointed by the council of war, the general, by warrant issued unto the lieutenant of the tribes,

demand the second essay, or such part of it as is decreed, whether by way of levy or recruit. That by the same warrant he appoint his time and rendezvous; that the several conductors of the tribes deliver him the forces demanded, at the time and place appointed. That, a general thus marching out with the standing army, a new army be elected out of the first essay as formerly, and a new general be elected by the senate; that so always there be a general sitting and a standing army, what generals or armies soever be marching. And that in case of invasion the bands of the elders be obliged unto like duty with those of the youth.

57. That an only son be discharged of these duties without prejudice. That of two brothers there be but one admitted to foreign service at one time. That of more brothers, not above half. That whoever otherwise refuseth his lot, except upon cause shown he be dispensed withal by the phylarch, or upon penitence be by them pardoned and restored, by such refusal be incapable of electing or being elected in this commonwealth; as also that he pay unto the state a fifth of his revenue for protection, besides taxes. That divines, physicians and lawyers, as also trades not at leisure for the essays, be so far forth exempted from this rule that they be still capable of all preferments in their respective professions, with indemnity, and without military education or service.

A commonwealth whose militia consisteth of mercenaries, to be safe, must be situated as Venice, but can in no wise be great. The industry of Holland is the main revenue of that state; whence, not being able to spare hands unto her arms, she is cast upon strangers and mercenary forces, through which we in our time have seen Amsterdam necessitated to let in the sea upon her, and to become (as it were) Venice. Unto a popular government that could not do the like, mercenary arms have never failed to be fatal; whence the last proposition is that which in every well-ordered commonwealth hath been looked unto as the main guard of liberty.

In this Israel was formidable beyond all other commonwealths with a kind of fulmination. Saul, when he heard the cruelty of Nahash the Ammonite, at the leaguer of Jabesh-Gilead,

> took a yoke of oxen and hewed them in pieces, and sent them throughout the coasts of Israel, by the hands of messengers, saying, whosoever cometh not out after Saul, and after Samuel, so shall it be done unto his oxen.

Which amounted not only unto a confiscation of goods (the riches of the Israelites lying most in their cattle) but unto a kind of anathema, as more plainly appeareth where it is said: Curse ye Meroz, curse ye bitterly the inhabitants thereof, because they came not forth to help the Lord against the mighty. Nay, this ἀορπατεια, desertion of the military orders and services, in Israel was sometimes punished with total extermination, as after the victory against Benjamin, where the congregation or political assembly of that people, making inquisition what one of the tribes of Israel came not up to the Lord in Mizpah (the place where, before the taking of Jerusalem, they held, as I may say, their parliaments) and finding that there came none to the camp from Jabesh-Gilead, sent thither twelve thousand men of the valiantest, saying, go and smite the inhabitants of Jabesh-Gilead with the edge of the sword, with the women and children; which was done accordingly.

But by this time men will shrink at this as a dreadful order, and begin to compute that a commonwealth, let her prerogatives for the rest be what they will, must at this rate be but a dear purchase; whereas indeed, if this way cost something, there is no other that doth not hazard all, forasmuch as, discarding this order, play your game as you can, you are sometime or other a prey to your enemies or to your mercenaries. This certainly is that root in the penetralia, the bowels of a commonwealth, whence never any court arts or polish could attain unto the gallantry of splendour of the education in popular governments. For let any man, remembering what it was to be a Gideon, a Miltiades, a Timoleon, a Scipio, or a magistrate in a commonwealth, consider, if there should be no way with us to magistracy but by having served three years at sea and three years at land, how the whole face and genius of education, both in the better and in the lower sort, would of necessity be changed in this nation, and what kind of magistrates such experience in those services must create unto the commonwealth. Consider whether the threatened punishments of this order, albeit through unacquaintance they may at the first sight have some brow, would not, as they have done in other commonwealths of like structure, even with low spirits, expire in scorn and contempt, or through the mere contemplation of the reward of honour, nay of the honour itself, in which point where right hath not been done, men, under governments of this nature, have been much more apt unto heats; as where the men of Ephraim fought against Jephtha, for an affront in this kind which they conceived him to have put upon them. Wherefore passed thou over to fight against the children of Ammon, and didst not call us to go with thee? We will burn thine house upon thee with fire.

Nor is this way so expensive of the purse or of blood. Not of the public purse, because it detesteth mercenaries; nor of the private purse, because the ways of education, thus directed, are all assisted with the state's pay, so that a man in this road might educate three children cheaper, and to the most solid ends, than he could any one unto trifles in those which among us hitherto have been usual. And as to blood, there is nothing more certain than that idleness, and her inseparable companion luxury, are exceedingly more wasteful, as of the purse so of health, nay and of life itself, than is war; which nevertheless this order is such as doth rather prevent than necessitate, in regard that to be potent in arms is the way of peace. But whereas in a martial commonwealth there may be men having exceeded the thirtieth year of their age, who like those of Ephraim would yet take it ill to be excluded the lists of honour, and it must also be unto the detriment of the commonwealth that they should; for these, whom we may call volunteers, it is proposed:

> 58. That upon warrants issued forth by the general for recruits or levies, there be an assembly of the phylarch in each tribe; that such volunteers, or men being above thirty years of age as are desirous of farther employment in arms, appear before the phylarch so assembled. That any number of these, not exceeding one moiety of the recruits or levies of that tribe, may be taken on by the phylarch,

so many of the youth being at the discretion of this council disbanded, as are taken one of the volunteers. That the levies thus made be conducted by the conductor of the respective tribe unto the rendezvous appointed. And that the service of these be without other term or vacation than at the discretion of the senate and the people, or such instructions unto the general, as shall by them in that case be provided.

Thus much for the military defensive part of this model. For offences in general it is written, <u>Woe unto the world because of offences; for it must needs be that offences come, but woe to that man by whom the offence cometh</u>. Among offences are offensive wars; now, it being out of question that, for the righteous execution of this woe upon him or them by whom the offence cometh, a war may be just and necessary, as also that victory in a just and necessary war may entitle one prince or one people unto the dominion or empire of another prince or people, it is also out of question that a commonwealth, unless in this case she be provided both to acquire and to hold what she acquireth, is not perfect;. . . .*

EDUCATION SYSTEM

The <u>twenty-sixth order</u>: instituting that if a parent have but one son, the education of that one son shall be wholly at the disposing of that parent, but whereas there be free schools erected and endowed, or to be erected and endowed in every tribe of this nation, to a sufficient proportion for the education of the children of the same; which schools, to the end that there be no detriment of hindrance unto the scholars upon case of removing from one unto another, are every of them to be governed by the strict inspection of the censors of the tribes, both upon the schoolmasters, their manner of life and teaching, and the proficiency of the children, after the rules and method of that in Hiera.+ If a parent have more sons than one, the censors of the tribes shall animadvert upon and

---

*The Art of Lawgiving.
+Westminster

punish him that sendeth not his sons within
the ninth year of their age unto some one of
the schools of a tribe, there to be kept and
taught if he be able at his charges, and if he
be not able gratis, till they arrive at the
age of fifteen years. And a parent may dispose of his sons at the fifteenth year of their
age, according unto his choice or ability,
whether it be unto service in the way of apprentices unto some trade or otherwise, or
unto farther study, as by sending them unto
the Inns of Court, of Chancery, or unto one
of the universities of this nation. But he
that taketh not upon him some one of the
professions proper unto some one of those
places, shall not continue longer in any of
them till they have /sic/ attained unto the
age of eighteen years; and every man having
not at that age of eighteen years taken
upon him, or addicted himself unto, the
profession of the law, theology or physic,
and being no servant, shall be capable of
the essay of the youth, and no other person
whatsoever; except a man, having taken upon
him such a profession, happen to lay it by
ere he arrive at three or four and twenty
years of age, and be admitted unto this
capacity by the respective phylarch, being
satisfied that he kept not out so long with
any design to evade the service of the
commonwealth, but that being no sooner at
his own disposing it was no sooner at his own
choice to come in. And if any youth or other
person of this nation have a desire to travel
into foreign countries upon occasion of business,
delight or farther improvement of his education,
the same shall be lawful for him upon a pass
obtained from the censors in parliament, putting a convenient limit unto the time and
recommending him unto the ambassadors, by
whom he shall be assisted and unto whom he
shall yield honour and obedience in their
respective residences. Every youth at his
return from his travel is to present the
censors with a paper of his own writing,
containing the interest of state or form of
government of the countries or some one of
the countries where he hath been; and if it
be good, the censors shall cause it to be

printed and published, prefixing a line in commendation of the author.

. . . .

Education by the first of the foregoing orders is of six kinds: at the school, in the mechanics, at the universities, at the inns of court or chancery, in travels, and in military discipline; some of which I shall touch, and some I shall handle.

That which is proposed for the erecting and endowing of schools throughout the tribes, capable of all the children of the same and able to give unto the poor the education of theirs gratis, is only matter of direction in a case of very great charity, as easing the needy of the charge of their children from the ninth to the fifteenth year of their age, during which time their work cannot be profitable, and restoring them when they may be of use, furnished with tools whereof there be advantages to be made in every work, seeing he that can read and use his pen hath some convenience by it in the meanest vocation; and it cannot be conceived but that which comes (though in small parcels) to the advantage of every man in his vocation must amount unto the advantage of every vocation, and so unto that of the commonwealth. Wherefore this is commended unto the charity of every wise-hearted and well-minded man to be done in time, and as God shall stir him up or enable him, there being such provision already in the case as may give us leave to proceed without obstruction.

Parents (under animadversion of the censors) are to dispose of their children at the fifteenth year of their age unto something; but what, is left, according to their abilities or inclination, in their own choice. This, with the many, must be unto the mechanics: that is to say, unto agriculture or husbandry, unto manufactures, or unto merchandise.

Agriculture is the bread of the nation; we are hung upon it by the teeth; it is a mighty nursery of strength, the best army and the most assured knapsack; it is managed with the least turbulent or ambitious, and the most innocent hands of all other arts. Wherefore I am of Aristotle's opinion, that a commonwealth of husbandmen (and such is ours) must be the best of all others. Certainly, my lords, you have no measure of what ought to be, but what can be done for the encouragement of this profession; I could wish I were husband good enough to direct something to this end; but racking of rents is a vile thing in the richer sort, an uncharitable one to the poorer, a mark of slavery, and nips your commonwealth in the fairest blossom. On the other side, if there should be too much ease given in this kind, it would occasion sloth, and so destroy industry, the nerve of a commonwealth. But if ought might be done to hold the balance even between these two, it would be a work in this nation equal unto that for which Fabius was called Maximus by the Romans.

In manufactures and merchandise the Hollander hath gotten the start of us; but at the long run it will be found that a people working upon a foreign commodity doth but farm the manufacture, and that it is entailed upon them only where the growth of it is native; as also that it is one thing to have the carriage of other men's goods, and another for a man to bring his own unto the best market. Wherefore, nature having provided encouragement for these arts in this nation above others where, the people growing, they of necessity must also increase, it cannot but establish them upon a far more sure and effectual foundation than that of the Hollanders. But their educations are in order unto the first things or necessities of nature: as husbandry unto the food, manufacture unto the clothing, and merchandise unto the purse of the commonwealth.

There be other things in nature which, being second as to their order, for their dignity and value are first, and such to which the other are but accommodations. Of this sort are especially these: religion, justice, courage, wisdom.

The education that answers unto religion in our government is that of the universities. Moses the divine legislator was not only learned in all the learning of the Egyptians, but took into the fabric of his commonwealth the learning of the Midianites in the advice of Jethro, and his foundation of an university, laid in the Tabernacle and finished in the Temple, became that pinnacle from whence all the learning in the world hath taken wing; as the philosophy of the Stoics from the Pharisees, that of the Epicureans from the Sadducees, and from the learning of the Jews, so often quoted by our Saviour and fulfilled in him, the Christian religion. Athens was the most famous university in her days and her senators, that is to say the

Aeropagites, were all philosophers. Lacedaemon (to speak truth), though she could write and read, was not very bookish. But who disputeth hence against universities, disputeth in the same argument against agriculture, manufacture and merchandise, every one of these having been equally forbidden by Lycurgus, not for itself (for if he had not been learned in all the learning of Crete, and well travelled in the knowledge of other governments, he had never made his commonwealth), but for the diversion which they must have given his citizens from their arms, who, being but few, if they had minded anything else, must have deserted the commonwealth. For Rome, she had $\underline{\text{ingenium par imperio}}$, was as learned as great, and held her college of augurs in much reverence. Venice hath taken her religion upon trust; Holland cannot tend it to be very studious; nor doth Switz mind it much; yet are they all addicted unto their universities. We cut down trees to build houses, but I would have somebody show me by what reason or experience the cutting down of an university should tend unto the setting up of a commonwealth. Of this I am sure, the perfection of a commonwealth is not to be attained unto without the knowledge of ancient prudence, nor the knowledge of ancient prudence without learning, nor learning without schools of good literature; and these are such as we call universities. Now though mere university learning of itself, be that which (to speak the words of Verulamius), 'crafty men condemn and simple men only admire, yet is it such as wise men have use of; for studies do not teach their own use, but that is a wisdom without and above them, won by observation. Expert men may execute, and perhaps judge of particulars one by one; but the general counsels, and the plots, and the marshalling of affairs, come best from those that are learned.' Wherefore, if you would have your children to be statesmen, let them drink all means of these fountains, where perhaps there was never any. But what though the water a man drinks be not nourishment? It is the $\underline{\text{vehiculum}}$ without which he cannot be nourished. Nor is $\underline{\text{religion}}$ less concerned in this point than government; for take away your universities, and in a few years you lose it.

. . . .

Wherefore your religion is thus settled; the universities are the seminars of that part which is national, by which means others withal safely may be permitted to follow the liberty of their consciences, in regard that however they behave themselves, the ignorance of the unlearned in this case cannot lose the religion nor disturb the government, which otherwise it would most certainly do. And the universities with their emoluments, as also the benefices of the whole nation, are to be improved by such augmentations as may make a very decent and comfortable subsistence for the ministry, which is neither to be allowed synods nor assemblies (but upon the occasion shown in the universities, they are consulted by the council for religion), suffered to meddle with affairs of state nor to be capable of any other public preferment whatsoever; by which means the interest of the learned can never come to corrupt your religion nor disturb your government, which otherwise it would most certainly do.

. . . .

My lords, if you know not how to rule your clergy, you will most certainly be like a man that cannot rule his wife; have neither quiet at home nor honour abroad. Their honest vocation is to teach your children at the schools and the universities, and the people in the parishes; and yours is concerned to see that they do not play the shrews. Of which parts consists the education of your commonwealth, so far forth as it regards religion.

To justice, or that part of it which is commonly executive, answers the education of the Inns of Court or Chancery. Upon which to philosophise requires a peculiar kind of learning that I have not. But they who take upon them any profession proper unto the educations mentioned, that is, theology, physic, law, are not at leisure for the essays. Wherefore, the essays being degrees whereby the youth commence for all magistracies, offices and honours in the parish, hundred, tribe, senate or prerogative, divines, physicians and lawyers, not taking these degrees, exclude themselves from all such magistracies, offices and honours. And whereas lawyers are likest to exact farther reason for this; they, growing up from the most gainful art at the bar unto those magistracies upon the bench which are continually appropriated to themselves, and not only endowed with the greatest revenues but held for life, have the least reason of all the rest to pretend unto any other; especially in an equal commonwealth, where accumulation of magistracy, or to take a person engaged by his profit unto the laws as they stand into the power which is legislative, and should keep them unto what they were or ought to be, were a solecism in prudence. It is true that the legislative power may have need of advice and assistance from the executive magistracy or such as are learned in the law; for which cause the judges are (as they have heretofore been) assistants in the senate. Nor, however, it came about, can I see any reason why a judge, being but an assistant, a lawyer, should be a member of a legislative council.

. . . .

Lycurgus, as I said, by being a traveller became a legislator; but in times when prudence was another thing. Nevertheless we may not shut out this part of education, in a commonwealth which will be herself a traveller, for those of this make have seen the world; especially because this (though it be not regarded in our times, when things being left to take their chance, it fares with us accordingly) is certain: no man can be a politician, except he be first an historian or a traveller; for except he can see what must be, or what may be, he is no politician. Now, if he have no knowledge in story, he cannot tell what is; but he that neither knoweth what hath been, nor what is, can never tell what must be or what may be. Furthermore, the embassies in ordinary, by our constitution, are the prizes of young men, more especially such as have been travellers. Wherefore they of these inclinations, having leave of the censors, owe them account of their time, and cannot choose but lay it out with some ambition of praise or reward, where both are open; whence you will have eyes abroad and better choice of public ministers, your gallants showing themselves not more unto the ladies at their balls, than unto your commonwealth at her academy, when they return from their travels.

But this commonwealth, being constituted more especially of two elements, arms and councils, driveth by a natural instinct at courage and wisdom, which he who hath attained is arrived at the perfection of human nature. It is true that these virtues must have some natural root in him that is capable of them; but this amounteth not unto so great a matter as some will have it. For if poverty make an industrious, a moderate estate a temperate, and a lavish fortune a wanton man, and this be the common course of things; wisdom is rather of necessity than inclination. And that an army which was meditating upon flight hath been brought by despair to win the field, is so far from being strange that like causes will evermore produce like effects. Wherefore this commonwealth driveth her citizens like wedges: there is no way with them but through, nor end but that glory whereof man is capable by art or nature. That the genius of the Roman families preserved itself throughout the line, as (to instance in some) that the Manlii were still severe, the Publicolae lovers and the Appii haters of the people, is attributed by Machiavel unto their education; nor, if interest might add unto the reason why the genius of a patrician was one thing and that of a plebeian another, is the like so apparent between different nations who, according unto their different educations, have yet as different manners. It was anciently noted and long confirmed by the French, that in their first assaults their courage was more than that of men, and for the rest less than that of women; which nevertheless, through the amendment of their discipline, we see to be otherwise. I will not say but that some man or nation, upon equal improvement of this kind, may be lighter than some other, but certainly education is the scale without which no man or nation can truly know his or her own weight or value. By our histories we can tell when one Marpesian /Scot/ would have beaten ten Oceaners /Britains/, and when one Oceaner would have beaten ten Marpesians. Mark Antony was a Roman, but how did that appear in the embraces of Cleopatra? You must have some other education for your youth; or they, like that passage, will show better in romance than true story.*

SUMMARY

PART I

For the civil part it is proposed:

    1. That the whole native or proper territory of Oceana (respect had unto the tax-roll, unto the number of people, and to the extent of territory) be cast, with as much exactness as can be convenient, into fifty precincts, shires or tribes.

    2. That all citizens, that is freemen or such as are not servants, be distributed into horse and foot; that such of them as have one hundred pounds a year in

*The Commonwealth of Oceana.

lands, goods or money, or above that proportion, be accounted of the horse, and all such as have under that proportion be accounted of the foot.

3. That all elders or freemen, being thirty years of age or upwards, be capable of civil administration; and that the youth, or such freemen as are between eighteen years of age and thirty, be not capable of civil administration, but of military only; in such manner as shall follow in the military part of the model.

4. That the elders resident in each parish annually assemble in the same, as for example, upon Monday next ensuing the last of December. That they then and there elect out of their number every fifth man, or one man out of every five, to be for the term of the year ensuing a deputy of that parish; and that the first and second so elected be overseers or presidents for the regulating of all parochial congregations, whether of the elders or of the youth, during the term for which they were elected.

5. That so many parishes, lying nearest together, whose deputies shall amount to one hundred or thereabouts, be cast into one precinct called the hundred; and that in each precinct called the hundred there be a town, village or place appointed to be the capital of the same.

6. That the parochial deputies elected throughout the hundred assemble annually, for example upon Monday next ensuing the last of January, at the capital of their hundred. That they then and there elect out of the horse of their number one justice of the peace, one juryman, one captain, one ensign, and out of the foot of their number one other juryman, one high constable, etc.

7. That every twenty hundreds, lying nearest and most conveniently together, be cast into one tribe or shire. That, the whole territory being after this manner cast into tribes or shires, some town, village or place be appointed unto every tribe or shire for the capital of the same; and that these three precincts, that is the parish, the hundred and the tribe or shire, whether the deputies thenceforth annually chosen in the parishes or hundreds come to increase or diminish, remain firm and unalterable forever, save only by act of parliament.

8. That the deputies elected in the several parishes, together with their magistrates and other officers both civil and military, elected in their several hundreds, assemble or muster annually, for example, upon Monday next ensuing the last of February, at the capital of their tribe or shire.

9. That the whole body thus assembled, upon the first day of the assembly, elect out of the horse of their number one high sheriff, one lieutenant of the tribe or shire, one custos rotulorum, one conductor and two censors. That the high sheriff be commander-in-chief, the lieutenant commander in the second place, and the conductor in the third, of this band or squadron. That the custos rotulorum be muster-master and keep the rolls. That the censors be governors of the ballot. And that the term of these magistrates be annual.

10. That the magistrates of the tribe, that is to say, the high sheriff, lieutenant, custos rotulorum, the censors and the conductor, together with the magistrates and officers of the hundred, that is to say, the twenty justices of the peace, the forty jurymen, the twenty high constables be one troop and one company apart, called the prerogative troop or company. That this troop bring in and assist the justices of assize, hold the quarter sessions in their several capacities, and perform their other functions as formerly.

11. That the magistrates of the tribe or shire, that is to say, the high sheriff, lieutenant, custos rotulorum, the censors and the conductors, together with the twenty justices elected at the hundreds, be a court for the government of the tribe, called the phylarch; and that this court proceed in all matters of government as shall from time to time be directed by act of parliament.

12. That the squadron of the tribe, upon the second day of their assembly, elect two knights and three burgesses out of the horse of their number, and four other burgesses out of the foot of their number. That the knights have session in the senate for the term of three years, and that the burgesses be of the prerogative tribe, or representative of the people, for the like term. That if, in case of death or expulsion, a place become void in the senate or popular assembly, the respective shire or tribe have timely

notice from the signory, and proceed in the manner aforesaid unto extraordinary election of a deputy or senator, for the remaining part of a term of the senator or deputy deceased or expelled.

13. That for the full and perfect institution at once of the assemblies mentioned, the squadron of each tribe or shire, in the first year of the commonwealth, elect two knights for the term of one year, two other knights for the term of two years, and lastly, two knights more for the term of three years; the like for the burgesses of the horse first, and then for those of the foot.

14. That a magistrate or officer elected at the hundred be thereby barred from being elected a magistrate of the tribe, or of the first day's election; that no former election whatsoever bar a man of the second day's election at the tribe, or to be chosen a knight or burgess. That a man being chosen a knight or burgess, who before was chosen a magistrate or officer of the hundred or tribe, delegate his former office or magistracy in the hundred or the tribe to any other deputy, being no magistrate nor officer, and being of the same hundred and of the same order, that is, of the horse or of the foot respectively. That the whole and every part of the foregoing orders for election in the parishes, the hundreds, and the tribes be holding and inviolate, upon such penalties in case of failure as shall hereafter be provided by act of parliament against any parish, hundred, tribe or shire, deputy or person so offending.

15. That the knights of the annual election in the tribes take their places on Monday next ensuing the last of March in the senate. That the like number of knights, whose session determineth at the same time, recede. That every knight or senator be paid out of the public revenue quarterly seventy-five pounds during the term of session, and be obliged to sit in purple robes.

16. That annually, upon reception of the new knights, the senate proceed unto election of new magistrates and counsellors. That for magistrates they elect one archon or general, one orator or speaker, and two censors, each for the term of one year, these promiscuously; and that they elect one commissioner of the great seal and one of the treasury, each for the term of three years, out of the new knights only.

17. That the archon or general and the orator or speaker, as consuls of the commonwealth and presidents of the senate, be, during the term of their magistracy, paid quarterly five hundred pounds; that the ensigns of these magistracies be a sword borne before the general, and a mace before the speaker; that they be obliged to wear ducal robes; and that what is said of the archon or general in this proposition be understood only of the general sitting and not of the general marching.

18. That the general sitting, in case he be commanded to march, receive field pay; and that a new general be forthwith elected by the senate to succeed him in the house, with all the rights, ensigns and emoluments of the general sitting; and this so often as one or more generals are marching.

19. That the three commissioners of the great seal, and the three commissioners of the treasury, using their ensigns and habit and performing their other functions as formerly, be paid quarterly unto each of them three hundred seventy-five pounds.

20. That the censors be each of them chancellor of one university by virtue of their election that they govern the ballot, that they be presidents of the council for religion; that they have, under appeal unto the senate, right to note and remove a senator that is scandalous; that each have a silver wand for the ensign of his magistracy, that each be paid quarterly three hundred seventy-five pounds, and be obliged to wear scarlet robes.

21. That the general sitting, the speaker and the six commissioners above-said be the signory of this commonwealth.

22. That there be a council of state consisting of fifteen knights, five out of each order or election; and that the same be perpetuated by the annual election of five out of the new knights or last elected into the senate.

23. That there be a council for religion consisting of twelve knights, four out of each order, and perpetuated by the annual election of four out of the knights last elected into the senate. That there be a council for trade consisting of a like number, elected and perpetuated in the same manner.

24. That there be a council of war, not elected by the senate, but elected by the council of state out of themselves. That this council of war consist of nine knights, three out of each order, and be perpetuated by the annual election of three out of the last knights elected into the council of state.

25. That in case the senate add nine knights more out of their own number unto the council of war, the said council be understood by such addition to be dictator of the commonwealth, for the term of three months and no longer, except by further order of the senate the said dictatorian power be prolonged for a like term.

26. That the signory have session and suffrage, with right also jointly or severally to propose both in the senate and in all senatorian councils.

27. That each of the three orders or divisions of knights in each senatorian council elect one provost for the term of one week; and that any two provosts of the same council so elected may propose unto the respective council, and not otherwise.

28. That some fair room or rooms, well furnished and attended, be allowed at the state's charge for a free and open academy unto all comers, at some convenient hour or hours towards the evening. That this academy be governed according to the rules of good breeding or civil conservation, by some or all of the proposers; and that in the same it be lawful for any man, by word of mouth or by writing, in jest or in earnest, to propose unto the proposers.

29. That for ambassadors in ordinary, there be four residences, as France, Spain, Venice and Constantinople; that every resident, upon election of a new ambassador in ordinary, remove to the next residence in the order nominated till, having served in them all, he return home. That upon Monday next ensuing the last of November, there be every second year elected by the senate some fit person, being under thirty-five years of age and not of the senate nor of the popular assembly; that the party so elected repair, upon Monday next ensuing the last of March following, as ambassador in ordinary unto the court of France, and there reside for the term of two years, to be computed from the first of April next ensuing his election. That every ambassador in ordinary be allowed three thousand

pounds a year during the term of his residences; and
that if a resident come to die, there be an extraordinary election into his residence for his term, and
for the remainder of his removes and progress.

30. That all emergent elections be made by scrutiny,
that is by a council, or by commissioners proposing and
by the senate resolving, in the manner following: that
all field officers be proposed by the council of war;
that all ambassadors extraordinary be proposed by the
council of state; that all judges and sergeants at law
be proposed by the commissioners of the great seal;
that all barons and officers of trust in the exchequer
be proposed by the commissioners of the treasury; and
that such as are thus proposed, and approved by the
senate by held lawfully elected.

31. That the congnizance of all matter of state be
considered, or law to be enacted, whether it be provincial or national, domestic or foreign, appertain
unto the council of state. That such affairs of either
kind as they shall judge to require more secrecy be
remitted by this council, and appertain unto the council
of war, being for that end a select part of the same.
That the cognizance and protection both of the national
religion and of the liberty of conscience equally
established, after the manner to be shown in the
religious part of this model, appertain unto the council
for religion. That all matter of traffic and regulation
of the same appertain unto the council for trade. That
in the exercise of these several functions, which
naturally are senatorian or authoritative only, no
council assume any other power than such only as shall
be estated upon the same by act of parliament.

32. That what shall be proposed unto the senate by
one or more of the signory or proposers general, or
whatever was proposed by any two of the provosts or
particular proposers unto their respective council and,
upon debate at that council, shall come to be proposed
by the same unto the senate, be necessarily debatable
and debated by the senate. That in all cases wherein
power is derived unto the senate by law made or by act
of parliament, the result of the senate be ultimate;
that in all cases of law to be made, or not already
provided for by act of parliament, as war and peace,
levy of men or money, or the like, the result of the
senate be not ultimate. That whatsoever is decreed
by the senate upon a case wherein their result is not

ultimate be proposed by the senate unto the prerogative tribe or representative of the people; except only in cases of such speed or secrecy wherein the senate shall judge the necessary slowness or openness in this way of proceeding to be of detriment or danger unto the commonwealth.

33. That if, upon the motion of proposition of a council or proposer general, the senate add nine knights, promiscuously chosen out of their own number, unto the council of war, the same council, as thereby made dictator, have power of life and death, as also to enact laws in all such cases of speed or secrecy, for and during the term of three months and no longer, except upon new order from the senate. And that all laws enacted by the dictator be good and valid for the term of one year and no longer, except the same be proposed by the senate and resolved by the people.

34. That the burgesses of the annual election returned by the tribes enter into the prerogative tribe, popular assembly or representative of the people, upon Monday next ensuing the last of March; and that the like number of burgesses whose term is expired, recede at the same time. That the burgesses thus entered elect unto themselves out of their own number two of the horse, one to be captain and the other to be cornet of the same; and two of the foot, one to be captain and the other to be ensign of the same; each for the term of three years. That these officers being thus elected, the whole tribe or assembly proceed to the election of four annual magistrates, two out of the foot to be tribunes of the foot, and two out of the horse to be tribunes of the horse. That the tribunes be commanders of this tribe in chief, so far as it is a military body, and presidents of the same as it is a civil assembly. And lastly, that this whole tribe be paid weekly, as followeth. Unto each of the tribunes of the horse seven pounds; unto each of the tribunes of foot six pounds; unto each of the captains of horse five pounds; unto each of the captains of foot four pounds; unto each of the cornets three pounds; unto each of the ensigns two pounds seven shillings; unto every horseman two pounds; and to every one of the foot, one pound ten shillings.

35. That inferior officers, as captains, cornets, ensigns, be only for the military discipline of this squadron or tribe. That the tribunes have session in the senate without suffrage; that they have session of

course and with suffrage in the dictatorian council, so
often as it is created by the senate. That they be
presidents of the court in all cases, to be judged by
the people; and that they have right, under an appeal
unto the popular assembly, to note or remove any
deputy or burgess that is scandalous.

36. That peculation or defraudation of the public,
as cases tending to the subversion of the government,
be tryable by this representative; and that there be
an appeal unto the same in all cases, and from all
magistrates, courts and councils, whether national or
provincial.

37. That the right of debate, as also of proposing
to the people, be wholly and only in the senate, without any power at all of result not derived from the
people.

38. That the power of result be wholly and only in
the popular assembly, without any right at all of debate.

39. That the senate, having debated and agreed
upon a law to be proposed, cause promulgation of the
same to be made for the space of six weeks before proposition; that is, cause the law to be printed and
published so long before it is to be proposed.

40. That, promulgation being made, the signory
demand of the tribunes being present in the senate an
assembly of the people. That the tribunes, upon such
demand by the signory or by the senate, be obliged to
assemble the prerogative tribe or representative of the
people in arms, by sound of trumpet, with drums beating
and colours flying, in any town, field or market place
being not above six miles distant, upon the day and at
the hour appointed, except the meeting through inconvenience of the weather, or the like, be prorogued by
consent of the signory and the tribunes. That, the
prerogative tribe being assembled accordingly, the
senate propose to them by two or more of the senatorian
magistrates, thereunto appointed at the first promulgation of the law. That the proposers for the senate
open unto the people the occasion, motives, and reasons
of the law to be proposed; and, the same being done,
put it by distinct clauses unto the ballot of the
people. That if any material clause or clauses be rejected by the people, they be reviewed by the senate,

altered and proposed (if they think fit) to the third
time, but no oftener.

41. That what is thus proposed by the senate, and
resolved by the people, be the law of the land, and no
other, except as in the case reserved unto the dictatorian council.

42. That every magistracy, office, or election
throughout this whole commonwealth, whether annual or
triennial, be understood of consequence to enjoin an
interval or vacation equal unto the term of the same.
That the magistracy of a knight and of a burgess be in
this relation understood as one and the same; and that
this order regard only such elections as are national
or domestic, and not such as are provincial or foreign.

43. That for an exception from this rule, where
there is but one elder of the horse in one and the same
parish, that elder be eligible in the same without interval; and where there be four elders of the horse
or above in one and the same parish, there be not under
two nor above half of them eligible at the same election.

44. That throughout all the assemblies and councils
of the commonwealth, the quorum consist of one half in
the time of health, and of one third part in a time of
sickness, being so declared by the senate.

PART 2

For the religious part it is proposed:

45. That the universities, being prudently re-
formed, be preserved in their rights and endowments for
and towards the education and provision of an able
ministry.

46. That the legal and ancient provision for the
national ministry be so augmented that the meanest sort
of livings or benefices, without defalcation from the
greater, be each improved to the revenue of one hundred
pounds a year at the least.

47. That, a benefice becoming void in any parish,
the elders of the same may assemble and give notice
unto the vice-chancellor of either university by certificate, specifying the true value of that benefice;
that the vice-chancellor, upon receipt of such cer-

tificate, be obliged to call a congregation of his
university; that the congregation of the university to
this end assembled, having regard unto the value of the
benefice, make choice of a person fitted for the ministerial function, and return him unto a parish by either
of the universities, exercise the office and receive
the benefits as minister of the parish for the term of
one year; that, the term of one year expired, the elders
of the parish assemble, and put the election of the probationer unto the ballot; that if the probationer have
three parts in four of the balls or votes in the affirmative, he be thereby ordained and elected minister
of that parish; not afterwards to be degraded or removed but by the censors of the tribe, the phylarch of
the same, or the council of religion in such cases as
shall be unto them reserved by act of parliament. That
in case the probationer come to fail of three parts in
four at the ballot, he depart from that parish; and if
he return unto the university, it be without diminution
of the former offices or preferments which he there enjoyed, or any prejudice unto his future preferment: and
that it be lawful in this case for any parish to send
so often to either university, and be the duty of either
vice-chancellor upon such certificates to make return
of different probationers, till such time as the elders
of that parish have fitted themselves with a minister
of their own choice and liking.

  48. That the national religion be exercised according to a directory in that case, to be made and
published by act of parliament. That the national
ministry be permitted to have no other public preferment or office in this commonwealth. That a national
minister, being convicted of ignorance or scandal, be
moveable out of his benefice by the censors of the tribe,
under an appeal unto the phylarch or to the council for
religion.

  49. That no religion being contrary unto or destructive of Christianity, nor the public exercise of
any religion being grounded upon or incorporated into
a foreign interest, be protected by or tolerated in
this state. That all other religions, with the public
exercise of the same, be both tolerated and protected
by the council of religion: and that all professors of
any such religion be equally capable of all elections,
magistracies, preferments and offices in this commonwealth, according unto the orders of the same.

PART 3

For the military part it is proposed:

50. That annually upon Wednesday next ensuing the last of December, the youth of each parish (under the inspection of the two overseers of the same) assemble and elect the fifth man of their number, or one in five of them, to be for the term of that year deputies of the youth of that parish.

51. That annually on Wednesday next ensuing the last of January, the said deputies of the respective parishes meet at the capital of the hundred (where there are games and prizes allotted for them, as hath been shown elsewhere); that there they elect to themselves out of their own number one captain and one ensign. And that of these games and this election, the magistrates and officers of the hundred be presidents and judges for the impartial distribution of the prizes.

52. That annually upon Wednesday next ensuing the last of February, the youth through the whole tribe thus elected be received at the capital of the same by the lieutenant as commander-in-chief, by the conductor and by the censors; that under inspection of these magistrates, the said youth be entertained with more splendid games, disciplined in a more military manner, and divided by lot unto sundry parts or essays, according to rules elsewhere given.

53. That the whole youth of the tribe thus assembled be the first essay. That out of the first essay there be cast by lot two hundred horse and six hundred foot; that they whom their friends will or themselves can mount be accounted horse, and the rest foot. That these forces, amounting in the fifty tribes to ten thousand horse and thirty thousand foot, be always ready to march at a week's warning; and that this be the second essay, or the standing army of the commonwealth.

54. That for the holding of each province, the commonwealth in the first year assign an army of the youth, consisting of seven thousand five hundred foot and one thousand five hundred horse. That for the perpetuation of these provincial armies or guards, there be annually, at the time and places mentioned,

cast out of the first essay of the youth in each tribe or shire, ten horse and fifty foot; that is, in all the tribes five hundred horse, and two thousand five hundred foot for Marpesia /Scotland/, the like for Panopea /Ireland/, and the like of both orders for the sea-guards, being each obliged to serve for the term of three years upon the state's pay.

55. That the senate and the people, or the dictator, having decreed or declared war, and the field officers being appointed by the council of war, the general, by warrant issued unto the lieutenants of the tribes, demand the second essay, or such part of it as it decreed, whether by way of levy or recruit. That by the same warrant he appoint his time and rendezvous; that the several conductors of the tribes or shires deliver him the forces demanded at the time and place appointed. That, a general thus marching out with the standing army, a new army be elected out of the first essay as formerly, and a new general be elected by the senate: that so always there be a general sitting and a standing army, what generals soever be marching. And that in case of invasion the bands of the elders be obliged unto like duty with those of the youth.

56. That an only son be discharged of these duties without prejudice. That of two brothers there be but one admitted to foreign service at one time. That of more brothers, not above half. That whoever otherwise refuseth his lot, except upon cause shown he be dispensed withal by the phylarch, or upon penitence he be by them pardoned and restored, by such refusal be incapable of electing or being elected in this commonwealth; as also that he pay unto the state a fifth of his revenue for protection, besides taxes. That divines, physicians and lawyers, as also trades not at leisure for the essays, be so far forth exempted from this rule that they be still capable of all preferments in their respective professions with indemnity.

57. That upon warrants issued forth by the general for recruits or levies, there be an assembly of the phylarch in each tribe; that such volunteers, or men being above thirty years of age as are desirous of farther employment in arms, appear before the phylarch so assembled. That any number of these, not exceeding one moiety of the recruits or levies of that tribe or shire, may be taken on by the phylarch, so many of the youth being at the discretion of this council disbanded as

are taken on of the volunteers. That the levies thus
made be conducted by the conductor of the respective
tribe or shire unto the rendezvous appointed. And that
the service of these be without other term or vacation,
than at the discretion of the senate and the people,
or such instructions unto the general as shall by them
in that case be provided.

PART 4

For the provincial part* it is proposed:

    58. That upon expiration of magistracy in the
senate, or at the annual recess of one third part of
the same, there be elected by the senate, out of the
part receding, into each provincial council four knights
for the term of three years, thereby to render each
provincial council (presuming it in the beginning to
have been constituted of twelve knights, divided after
the manner of the senate by three several lists or
elections) of annual, triennial and perpetual revolution
or rotation.

    59. That out of the same third part of the senate
annually receding, there be unto each province one
knight elected for the term of one year. That the
knight so elected be the provincial archon, general
or governor. That a provincial archon, governor or
general, receive annually in April, at his rendezvous
appointed, the youth or recruits elected in the pre-
cedent month to that end by the tribes, and by their
conductors delivered accordingly. That he repair with
the said youth and recruits unto his respective province, and there dismiss that part of the provincial
guard or army whose triennial term is expired. That
each provincial governor have the conduct of affairs of
war and of state in his respective province, with advice of the provincial council; and that he be president of the same.

    60. That each provincial council elect three
weekly proposers or provosts, after the manner and to
the ends already shown in the constitution of senatorian councils; and that the provost of the senior list,
during his term, be president of the council in absence
of the provincial archon or general.

*Scotland and Ireland.

61. That each provincial council proceed according unto instructions received from the council of state, and keep intelligence with the same by any two of their provosts, for the government of the province as to matter of war or of state. That upon levies of native or proper arms by the senate and the people, a provincial council (having unto that end received orders) make levies of provincial auxiliaries accordingly. That auxiliary arms upon no occasion whatsoever exceed the proper or native arms in number. That for the rest, the provincial council maintain the provincials - defraying their peculiar guards and council by such known proportion of tributes as on them shall be set by the senate and the people - in their proper rights, laws, liberties and immunities, so far forth as, upon the merits of the cause whereupon they were subdued, it seemed good unto the senate and the people to confirm them. And that it be lawful for the provincials to appeal from their provincial magistrates, councils or generals to the people of Oceana.*

*The Rota.

CHAPTER IV

APPENDIX

"The right constitution, coherence and proper symmetry of a form of government goeth for the greater part upon invention . . . . Invention is most perfect in one man."

                              Aphorisms Political

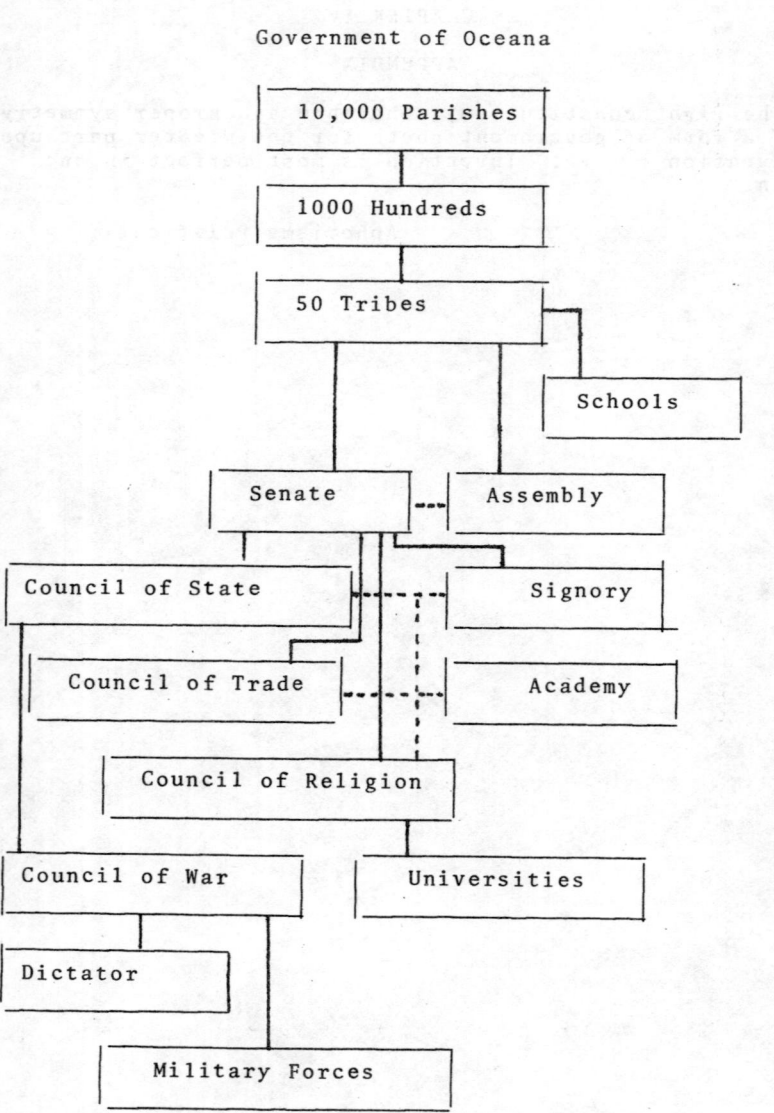

W. Calvin Dickinson

A professor at Tennessee Technological University, Dickinson earned the Ph.D. in history of England at the University of North Carolina (1967), studying with Stephen Baxter. His publications are numerous in both English and U.S. history.